A User's Manual for the Aging Voice

A User's Manual for the Aging Voice

Martha Howe

With contributions by Karen Brunssen,
Barbara Fox DeMaio, Lisa Popeil, Sharon L. Radionoff,
Martha L. Randall, Brenda Smith, Jennifer Trost

This edition first published 2020 © 2020 by Compton Publishing Ltd.

Registered office: Compton Publishing Ltd, 30 St. Giles', Oxford, OX1 3LE, UK

Registered company number: 07831037

Editorial offices: 35 East Street, Braunton, EX33 2EA, UK

Web: www.comptonpublishing.co.uk

The right of the authors to be identified as the authors of this work has been asserted in accordance with the UK Copyright, Designs and Patents Act 1988.

All rights reserved. No part of this publication may be reproduced, stored in a retrieval system, or transmitted, in any form or by any means, electronic, mechanical, photocopying, recording or otherwise, except as permitted by the UK Copyright, Designs and Patents Act 1988, without the prior permission of the publisher.

Trademarks: Designations used by companies to distinguish their products are often claimed as trademarks. Any brand names and product names used in this book are trade names, service marks, trademarks or registered trademarks of their respective owners. The publisher is not associated with any product or vendor mentioned in this book.

Disclaimer: This book is designed to provide helpful information on the subject discussed. This book is not meant to be used, nor should it be used, to diagnose or treat any medical condition. For diagnosis or treatment of any medical condition, consult your own physician. The publisher and author are not responsible for any specific medical condition that may require medical supervision and are not liable for any damages or negative consequences to any person reading or following the information in this book. References are provided for informational purposes only and do not constitute endorsement of any product, website, or other source.

Permissions: Where necessary, the publisher and author(s) have made every attempt to contact copyright owners and clear permissions for copyrighted materials. In the event that this has not been possible, the publisher invites the copyright owner to contact them so that the necessary acknowledgments can be made.

ISBN 978-1-909082-61-8

A catalogue record for this book is available from the British Library.

Cover design: David Siddall, http://www.davidsiddall.com

Cover image: Sean McCormac

Set in 11pt Adobe Caslon Pro by Regent Typesetting Ltd

1 2020

Contents

Acknowledgements	ix
About the Authors	xi
Introduction by Martha Howe	xvii
1. What's under the hood? *Martha Howe*	1
2. Gender differences, similarities, and transitions overview *Martha Howe*	5
3. The menopausal voice – singing through the storm *Barbara Fox DeMaio*	7
4. Options and pesky side effects *Martha Howe*	27
5. Back to the studio *Karen Brunssen*	37
6. Structural maintenance and aerobic breath *Martha Howe*	47
7. The aging voice: one singer's perspective *Martha L. Randall*	59
8. Aging, HRT, and stabilizing the voice *Lisa Popeil*	71
9. Hearing, sliding pitch, wobble and hitting the gravel *Martha Howe*	77
10. Vibrato and the older singer *Brenda Smith, DMA*	91
11. New normals *Sharon L. Radionoff*	107

12. Singing, your brain and memory – Alzheimer's, Parkinson's
    and Neurogenics   131
    Martha Howe

13. Reinventing the female classical voice after menopause   135
    Jennifer Trost

14. Keep singing and pay attention to your speaking   149
    Martha Howe

This book is dedicated
to everyone whose voice has gone rogue
at one time or another.

Acknowledgements

First and foremost, I wish to acknowledge Noel McPherson for bringing the idea of this book to my attention, and then his endless patience as I slowly pulled it together. In the same breath, my heartfelt thanks go out to the wonderful (and also quite patient) contributing authors:

Barbara Fox DeMaio, PhD, was the first to send me her chapter, compiled from her doctoral thesis studying the research on the effects of menopause. Her thesis, which she kindly and generously shares, has entered that golden land of being a major source document in the field. Karen Brunssen amazingly pulled her chapter together while touring the world with NATS National and learning the multi-faceted, consuming job of President of NATS and also publishing her own book, *The Evolving Singing Voice* with Plural Publishing. It has been a great joy to get to know the vibrant, ever resourceful Lisa Popeil and to have time to sit and share ideas with her during breaks at a NATS conference.

Sharon L. Radionoff, PhD, Martha L. Randall, and Brenda Smith, DMA, are gifts to my life from The Voice Foundation symposia. I am honored that these wonderful women have shared their fascinating, extensive knowledge and experience in the field. And last, but certainly not least, thanks to Jennifer Trost who kindly expanded upon a workshop she and Mary Saunders Barton presented at the 2016 NATS National Conference in Chicago on retraining for the demands of evolving repertoire.

I also wish to acknowledge two women who were interested in writing chapters, but who died suddenly and unexpectedly before we could pull it together. Pauline Tweed was a preacher's daughter and sang beautifully from her infancy to her hospital bed in her eighties, continually praising God and sharing her brilliant light, humor, love, and energy. She was an inspiring teacher, wonderful performer in multiple genres, and the mainstay of many a soprano section. A firm believer in 'Use It or Lose It', she warmed up for twenty minutes each day before teaching. Singing with her was a lovely, inspiring thing to do and after spending time with her, my step always felt lighter, and my own light brighter.

Tara Yvonne Potter was my dear friend for over half a century. We met while singing together in the alto section, and she went on to become a pharmacist, a chiropractor, and an energy healer. She was going to explain how our thoughts and actions imprint into our muscles, bones, and energy meridians and can cause blockages and areas of tension. These become our new 'normal' and can cause many different kinds of problems. I have covered some of that in my chapters, pulling from what I learned from her and her journey. I miss her insights, wisdom, and company.

And I deeply appreciate the encouragement and support from my sister and her husband, Dimaris and Art, my son Mark, his wife Amy, my three inspiring grandkids Hannah, Michael and Jack, and all my wonderful friends that helped me move through bouts of prescription-side-effect induced brain fog, grief, several huge moves, rogue knees, and the vocal changes that come with mid-sixties and beyond.

This has been a fascinating process for me, I have learned a great deal along the way, and again, thank you Noel for inviting me on this journey!

Martha Howe, Vienna 2019

About the Authors

Martha Howe

After an extensive performance path beginning with folk and church music, passing through the baroque, concert work and over fifty recitals, landing squarely in Wagner, Strauss and 20th–21st century opera, with over a hundred roles on major stages, Martha Howe began teaching voice and acting while singing in a Musicals school in Vienna, before returning to the U.S. in 2007. She moved back to Vienna at the end of 2018. Her stylistically wide-ranging studio includes Skype students in Europe and the U.S., and she coaches business people on their presentation skills.

Attending her first Symposium in 2011 was a revelatory experience. She found it fascinating to discover the science behind the vocal traditions. Vocally and technically, things were coming full circle. In 1907, Maude Douglas Tweedy stopped her concert career and began to work with Dr. Frank E. Miller, the leading laryngologist in New York City. By 1912, she had her regular studio of professional singers and was also what would be known today as Dr. Miller's Singing Health Specialist, working with his patients to clear vocal injuries while retraining them to prevent future injuries. Mme. Tweedy died in 1985, at the age of 98, after 70 years of teaching. Martha was one of Tweedy's last students. She then worked with master teacher Jane Randolph (presently at the San Francisco Conservatory) who inherited and refined Mme. Tweedy's technique. So it is not surprising that the science has only supported and clarified, never contradicted, this technique.

Martha has been writing for publication since 1998 and received a Master of Arts in Literature through the British Open University in 2008. In 2015, her book on the tumultuous beginnings of voice science, *Broadening the Circle, the history and future of The Voice Foundation*, was published by Compton Publishing on behalf of The Voice Foundation. You are invited to visit her website: marthahowe.com

Karen Brunssen

Karen Brunssen is Associate Professor of Music at the Bienen School of Music, Northwestern University in Evanston, Illinois where she teaches voice and is Co-Chair of Music Performance. She is a recipient of the Excellence in Teaching Award, and is a frequent teacher, clinician, and adjudicator for organizations, colleges, and universities throughout the United States, Canada, and Europe. Her presentations chronicle how changes in respiration, vibration and resonance impact realistic, age appropriate expectations for singing throughout a lifetime. She has done teaching residencies at Cambridge University, returns regularly to teach at the Zürcher Sing-Akademie in Switzerland, has presented or been a panelist for NATS, Opera America, ACDA, IFCM, NCCO, and Chorus America, and taught at the International Institute of Vocal Arts in Italy, and the Castleton Music Festival.

She began her two-year term as president of the National Association of Teachers of Singing in June 2018, has served as a Master Teacher for the NATS Intern Program, was 2016 NATS National Conference Program Chair, Governor of Central Region NATS, President of Chicago Chapter NATS, and is a member of the American Academy of Teachers of Singing.

Her busy singing career spanned over thirty years throughout the US and Europe. She received her undergraduate degree from Luther College and has done graduate work at Yale University and Kent State University. In 2013 she was presented with the Weston Noble Award by Luther College. Karen is the author of *The Evolving Singing Voice, Changes Across the Lifespan* (Plural Publishing, 2018)

Barbara Fox DeMaio

American Soprano, Barbara Fox DeMaio, has a deserved international fame. Her vast repertoire includes all the great roles of a Puccini and Verdi soprano, performed in theatres in Italy, Switzerland, Germany and France; Tosca, Lady Macbeth, Turandot, Aida, Abigaille in *Nabucco*, and also Amelia in *Ballo in Maschera*, Elvira in *Ernani*, Lucrezia in *I Due Foscari*, Leonora in *La Forza del Destino* and Odabella in La Scala's *Attila* directed by Riccardo Muti. She is also a noted interpreter of Norma, the Bellini heroine. Since returning to the United States she has added new shows to her repertoire; Bolcom's *Medea* and Hoiby's *Bon Appetit!* as well as the Witch in Humperdinck's *Hansel and Gretel*, Domina in *Forum*, Mama Rose in *Gypsy*, Grandma Helene in *Freaky Friday* and Costanza in the play *Enchanted April*.

DeMaio is currently an Asst. Prof. of Voice at the University of Central Oklahoma, teaching both Opera and Musical Theatre styles, Executive Director of Painted Sky Opera and a Level III Somatic Voicework© teacher. In October 2016, she was honored to be named as a Member Laureate by Sigma Alpha Iota. Her DMA Vocal pedagogy degree at Shenandoah University included dissertation research on the effect of menopause on the elite singing voice that she has since presented in the form of workshops and presentations across the US, and also in October 2017, at La Voce Artistica in Ravenna, Italy.

Lisa Popeil

Lisa Popeil, MFA in Voice, is one of LA's top voice coaches with over 50 years of voice study and 40 years of professional teaching experience. She is the creator of the Voiceworks® Method, Total Singer DVD, Daily Vocal Workout for Pop Singers CDs, is a co-author of the book *Sing Anything – Mastering Vocal Styles*, conducts voice research, and is an international lecturer and vocal health consultant. In addition, Lisa is on the Advisory Board of The Voice Foundation, an organization dedicated to 'Care of the Professional Voice' and is a voting member of NARAS, (the Grammy organization) ASCAP, SAG/AFTRA and the National Association of Teachers of Singing. She has contributed to *The Oxford Handbook of Singing*, *The Oxford Handbook of Music Education*, the "Journal of Voice" and the "Journal of Singing". Her interests focus on analysis of vocal genres, the mechanism of healthy belting, Contemporary Commercial Voice and vocal health strategies for touring professionals.

Ms. Popeil's extensive experience as a performer, recording artist, session singer, songwriter, musician and teacher makes her the go-to vocal consultant in Los Angeles. Her celebrity clientele includes singers from TV, film, Broadway and the pop music world. www.popeil.com

Sharon L. Radionoff, PhD

Dr. Radionoff had early exposure to many kinds of music through church/community choirs, concert/marching band as well as piano study and performance. Her love for music and teaching grew as she studied music in college. Although voice was her main instrument, she continued studies of trombone and piano and performed in recitals, operas, musicals, choirs, bands and orchestras. Upon graduating with her BME from Eastern Michigan University, she became a Middle School/High School band director. During this time, she attended an MENC conference at the University of Michigan where she heard Dr. Robert T. Sataloff lecture on "Care of the Professional Voice." This one lecture fueled her passion and changed the course of her life and, as they say, 'the rest is history.' This passion provoked her into knowing not just how to get desired vocal results but what allows these results to occur in the healthiest way. This zeal for voice care continued through her master's degree study at Southern Methodist University in Dallas and upon graduation she taught a variety of choirs, directed musicals and taught a full studio of voice students at Co-Lin Jr. College and then Southwestern Michigan College. She also directed community and church choirs.

Six years after their initial meeting, Dr. Sataloff invited her to complete a professional fellowship at the American Institute for Voice and Ear Research in Philadelphia, PA. Post fellowship and Ph.D coursework, she became the singing voice specialist at the Texas Voice Center with Dr. C. Richard Stasney. While there she conducted her dissertation research and was awarded her Ph.D. from Michigan State University in 1996. She has taught undergraduate and graduate vocal pedagogy, vocal pathways and studio voice students at University of Houston and vocal pedagogy at Rice University. Currently she is Singing Voice Specialist and Director of the Sound Singing Institute as well as being a Voice Care Team Member at the Texas Voice Center.

As a Singing Voice Specialist, Dr. Radionoff has a unique viewpoint in the field of Arts Medicine. Her education and experience as both teacher and performer as well as her motivation to know the why and the how, have created a platform of practical knowledge which enables her to empower singers to find healing and fulfilment.

Dr. Radionoff may be contacted at the Sound Singing Institute, www.SoundSinging.com.

Martha L. Randall

Martha Randall, (Soprano, B.M., M.M. from the University of Kansas, Fulbright Scholar), attended her first Symposium for the Care of the Professional Voice in 1976 and has been a regular attendee since that time. A student of Todd Duncan for many years, she teaches voice and voice pedagogy at the University of Maryland in College Park. She also maintains a small private studio and works with both amateur and professional singers. She has appeared at the Kennedy Center, Constitution Hall, the Phillips Gallery, and performed with the National Symphony, Washington Bach Consort, and Kansas City Philharmonic. Former students have appeared at the Met, Covent Garden, New York City Opera, Glimmerglass and Central City. She was president of NATS from 2006-08 and at the 2014 NATS Conference in Boston, collaborated with Physical Therapist Jodi Barth and Gincy Stezar, PTA, in a pre-conference workshop. She is a member of the American Academy of Teachers of Singing, now serving as chair. She collaborated with Jodi Barth and Gincy Stezar at the 2012 and 2013 Voice Foundation Symposiums.

She was on the faculty of the Voice Pedagogy Institute at Westminster Choir College in July of 2014 and was an invited participant and discussion leader on teaching language, diction, communication, and artistry for a Pedagogy Summit at Ohio State University in 2015. Email mrandal@umd.edu

Brenda Smith

Dr. Brenda Smith, DMA, a lyric soprano, teaches studio voice, singer's diction, and vocal pedagogy at the University of Florida in Gainesville, FL. She is widely recognized for her contributions to the concept of lifelong singing through proper voice care. She works regularly as a consultant, clinician, and conductor of amateur and professional choirs. She has collaborated with Dr. Robert T. Sataloff on a variety of projects to promote vocal health through choral singing. Dr. Smith and Dr. Sataloff have co-authored two textbooks that unite voice science, vocal pedagogy with choral conducting. (Choral Pedagogy, 3rd ed. and Choral Pedagogy and the Older Singer). In recognition of demonstrated excellence in teaching and her interest in voice science, Dr. Smith received the Van

Lawrence Fellowship in 2000, presented by the Voice Foundation and the National Association of Teachers of Singing.

Jennifer Trost

Associate Professor, Jennifer Trost joined the Penn State School of Music voice faculty in 2005 and is currently the coordinator of the Voice Area. Trost earned a BA in Music Education at Albion College in Michigan, a MM in Applied Voice at Michigan State University, and took advanced courses at the doctoral level at the University of Southern California. Prior to Penn State, she taught studio voice at the University of California in Santa Barbara, and the Richard Strauss Conservatory in Munich, Germany.

Trost is a young-dramatic soprano with a fifteen-year career as an opera singer. She spent two years with Los Angeles Opera as a resident artist; four years with the Wuppertal Opera in Wuppertal, Germany; and nine years with the Bavarian State Opera in Munich, Germany. She was privileged to work regularly with well-known conductors such as Lorin Maazel, Wolfgang Sawallisch, James Levine and, especially, Zubin Mehta, the General Music Director of the Bavarian State Opera.

From 2016–2018, Trost toured nationally with Judith Cloud's *Beethoven's Slippers: A Monodrama*; a one-woman show that she commissioned for this express purpose. She performed the work in both the piano quartet and piano/voice versions.

Introduction

Somewhere in the fifth or sixth decade of life, we start to notice that our body is just not letting us get away with as much any longer. Things we used to push through before suddenly start to push back. If you want to avoid the weaker, scratchier, old-person speaking voice, sing regularly. Singing, just like exercise, becomes much more important as the decades roll on. It will help maintain your ability to use your breath efficiently and effectively and keep more warmth and energy in your speaking voice.

In my late fifties, I had a group of Ave Marias scheduled on an upcoming recital and the various opening /a/s were all giving me grief. When did 'that' start? Why was that happening? A week before the performance date I had a serious conversation with myself; 'Martha, this isn't just because you're not warmed up, this keeps happening, and you have to deal with it NOW or you and the audience are in for a rough ride.' That was my personal introduction to what I now call 'hitting the gravel'. I had officially entered that phase of singing and of life where I had to really start paying attention to what my body and voice needed in the moment.

Each body has its own strengths and vulnerabilities, and each voice has its individual timing and responses. This book is a gathering together of experiences from a group of respected pedagogues and clinicians who let the reader in on what they do in their studios when working with older voices. You are welcome to take what you find useful from all the vocalises and tips and see how they work in your own experience.

The first chapters lead us through how the aging process affects every voice, plus the hormonal effects of menopause on the body and voice. Then we look at the impact on the voice of some common ailments and their medications, asking 'What should we look for?', 'What should be monitored?', 'Do I have a choice?'

The next chapters look at what to do about the changes in overall posture and strength, physical and vocal flexibility, and offer information on stabilizing the voice, excess vibrato, breath, maintaining your range, reestablishing the joy in singing, and keeping a strong speaking voice.

Finally, we look at the opportunities presented to keep singing through changing repertoire, evolving our expectations, finding new solutions, and enjoying new vocal territory.

Whether or not you consider yourself to be a singer, singing is one of the healthiest things you can do for yourself as the decades progress. It doesn't matter if you sing in your shower or in your car, if you are a karaoke star, sing on stage, or serenade yourself while cooking or working on projects, perform recitals, or participate in choirs. Fill your lungs with air, and sing. It has wide-reaching health benefits for everyone, including improved pulmonary function, the release of oxytocin, serotonin, dopamine, and endocannabinoids, plus increased production of immunoglobulin to boost your immune system and fight infections. You might notice that you have less need of pain medications, better concentration, and fewer symptoms of depression. It will keep your speaking voice strong and clear. All of this together means that singing, in whatever form works for you, helps brighten your outlook on life.

Hopefully this book will assist you to enjoy your aging voice more, communicate more easily, and make music longer than you thought possible. Why not expand your range in your eighties? Explore new modes of expression in your nineties? Sing your way into a century?

With the right care, and knowing what to expect down the road, you can keep your voice as long as you wish and help others extend their vocal range and abilities.

Martha Howe, Vienna, 2019

1

What's under the hood?

Martha Howe

Singing can feel like a magic act because it happens primarily in the autonomic system, the one we don't directly control. So, although there is a robust body of vocal science around singing and speech, when it comes to the act of singing, this knowledge however helpful it may be, gives way to imagery, feeling, and experiencing. During the decades I was performing, I had a mistrust of 'too much science', thinking that it was all well and good but didn't directly relate to what I was doing in rehearsal and performance. Much like just wanting my car to work, but not wanting to know the mysteries under the hood.

However, as my car gets older, it can be very helpful to understand what is making it clunk, how serious the clunk is, and how to keep it from shuddering at high speeds. So, let us 'lift the hood' on this instrument that allows us to communicate and to make music, and keep it running as smoothly as possible for as long as possible.

These illustrations are for reference when structural terms are used in the following chapters. First, a simple drawing of the larynx with the major elements identified. This view is directly from the front. You can think of the "V" shape in the center of the thyroid cartilage as the bit that can be seen in men as the 'Adam's Apple' (Fig. 1).

The next image is the back of the larynx (Fig. 2) as though looking through the back of the neck. You can see all the muscles that move the vocal folds that are protected by the thyroid cartilage and not visible from the front.

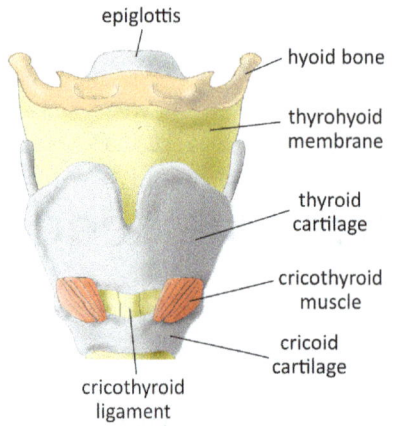

Figure 1. The larynx viewed from the front. Image copyright N Harrison and A Watson (2020) *A Singer's Guide to the Larynx* (reproduced with permission)

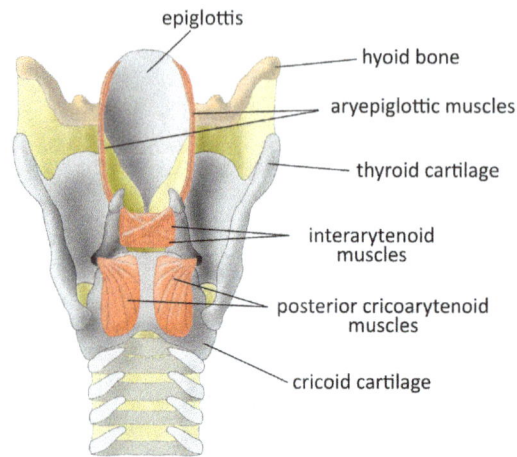

Figure 2. The larynx viewed from behind. Image copyright N Harrison and A Watson (2020) *A Singer's Guide to the Larynx* (reproduced with permission)

Then we have a view of the vocal folds from above (Fig. 3), looking down on the vocal folds, which are at the entrance to the trachea and keep food and liquid from entering the lungs when they are not being employed to make sound. Finally, a side view of the head (Fig. 4) to see where the larynx sits in the throat.

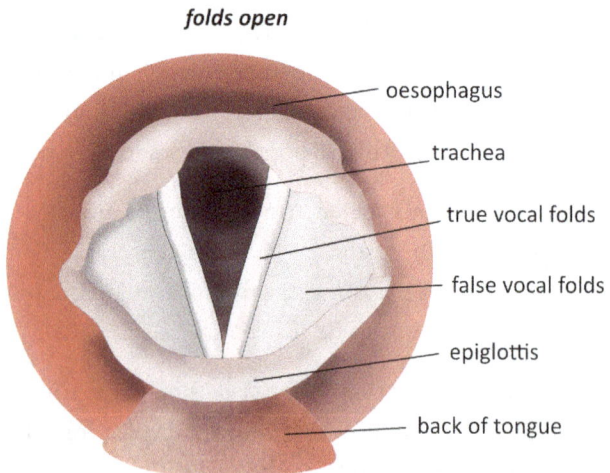

Figure 3. The vocal folds viewed from above.
Image copyright N Harrison and A Watson (2020)
A Singer's Guide to the Larynx (reproduced with permission)

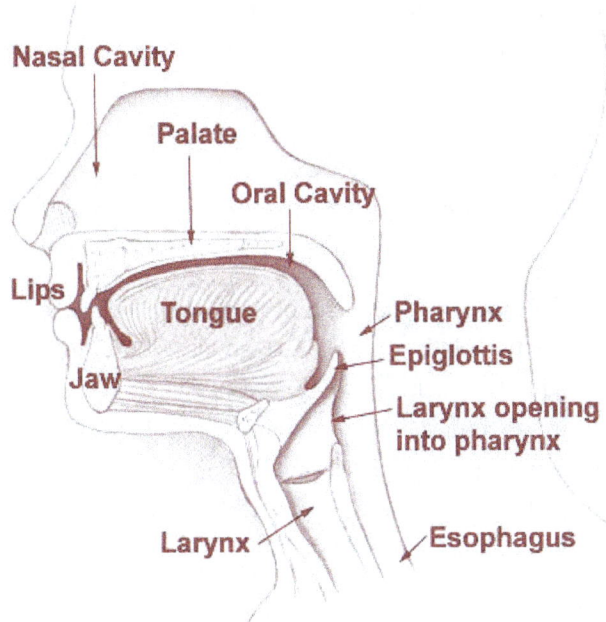

Figure 4. Side view of the head and neck showing
the position of the larynx in the neck

Does it feel like your larynx is changing? It is.

When we are born, our larynges are up behind our noses before they begin their journey after the first three months and for the next three years down into the throat. Then there are major changes for both males and females during puberty in the size of the larynx, length of the vocal folds and the vocal tract (the 'tube' from the vocal folds through the throat and mouth to the lips). This cascade of hormones at puberty also triggers the structure of the vocal folds themselves to change, with the epithelium dividing into three parts. Small wonder that male voices go through such drastic changes and female voices can be breathy one day and not the next, as everything in the larynx works to find balance in a continually morphing environment.

Ossification of the laryngeal cartilages

Tradition and perceived wisdom maintain that you finally get your full voice at around the age of thirty-two, especially larger voices, with the voice growing in strength into your late forties and fifties. From then on, its anyone's guess if the voice will hold or start to deteriorate, often depending on technique, use and abuse, practicing, and adaptability as the vocal coping mechanisms we've developed in our youth stop working so well. The science behind this timeline is the slow process of the structures of the larynx turning from cartilage to bone. The hyoid cartilage begins to ossify (become bone) at the age of two, as the larynx is descending. This is necessary as so many muscles are anchored to the hyoid and the larynx hangs from the hyoid. It has also been noted that our entire breathing apparatus, bronchi and lungs, hang from the larynx.

After the hormonal cascade of puberty, in the twenties the cricoid and thyroid cartilages begin to ossify. This is a slow process, taking around forty years, working from the front around to the back. The arytenoid cartilages join the process during the thirties. This ossification strengthens a voice during the thirties and forties, giving you the feeling that you can sing or speak 'bigger, louder, longer'. There will be a trade-off of loss of flexibility in bigger, heavier voices and in those who don't keep working on flexibility and agility.

Luckily, the cuneiform and corniculate cartilages on the thyroid cartilage, which are important for producing pitch and sound, are the last to ossify. In general, the laryngeal skeleton ossifies by around sixty-five in both men and women.

This is a growing challenge to singers and speakers, as the entire laryngeal structure and finally those very important tiny joints producing pitch and sound continue to harden, affecting flexibility and range. The aging process causes changes not only in the laryngeal cartilages, but also with the breakdown of collagen fibers, and changes in the cricoarytenoid joint surface, which becomes rougher. Plus, there are changes in the strength and flexibility of the muscles in the inner parts of the larynx, the covering of the vocal folds, and how quickly the nerves tell the larynx what to do. This process can be frustrating when it feels like nothing works as well, but an up-side is that it is rare for an older person to develop nodes, polyps, or hemorrhages on their vocal folds.

It is good to know what is going on as your speaking and singing voice changes over time. For example, gravity works on the throat and its muscle tone, so it becomes harder for the epiglottis to keep food and liquid out of the 'wrong tube'. Therefore, it is important to help the epiglottis by keeping your neck in good alignment when you eat. If you don't, you may have trouble swallowing and quite possibly, could cough more than you would like to during a meal.

These are cause and effect issues. When you understand more of the causes, the effects are not as surprising and there is a better chance of dealing with them directly, rather than thinking that your voice is falling apart on you. The following chapters have excellent tips and information on what to do about these changes and how to adapt to your new normal.

2

Gender differences, similarities, and transitions overview

Martha Howe

The information in this book applies to male, female, and transitional bodies. The physical changes in the larynx, voice, mind, nerves, muscles, and throughout the body due to aging are true for **all** bodies as they age. The slow changing of the cartilages in the larynx to bone happens to everyone over time. Male bodies have been found to have more ossification at the front of the thyroid cartilage than female bodies, so the peak that forms the male Adam's apple is stiffer, which is possibly an evolutionary protective device.

Even the effects of changing hormone levels are not that different between genders. When male hormones, androgens, are introduced into a body, they lower the overall pitch of a voice. This is true of all bodies. The cascade of androgens at puberty causes the male voice to drop in pitch. After menopause, female bodies are no longer producing the estrogen that was countering the small amount of progesterone (an androgen) produced each month, so the female voice may drift down over time. Females should be aware that androgen supplements will definitely lower their voice. When a person in a female body is transitioning to a male body, these androgens are a blessing. If you depend upon your higher range for singing or speaking, you will want to avoid them.

It has been noticed that older male voices tend to rise in pitch. Although there is a gradual lessening in testosterone in the later decades, the research on the reasons for the rise in pitch point more toward muscle-mass weakening in the vocal folds and surrounding muscles, plus pulmonary insufficiency. So weaker muscles in the larynx, thinner vocal folds, and not making the best use of the lungs are why older men's voices start to rise.

Androgens will lower a voice, but estrogen won't raise the overall pitch of a voice. Boys' and girls' voices are very hard to tell apart, and they have the same ranges, so we all started with a typical female range. The overall pitch of adult male and female voices is the result of the dimensions of the throat and length of the vocal folds. Simply put, once a voice has dropped due to androgens, be it a male or female voice, it will stay there.

People in male bodies transitioning to female bodies will sometimes wish to raise the overall pitch of their voice. Surgery has not proven to be a very effective nor a long-lasting solution. What is recommended instead, is to work with a Speech Language Pathologist on tone and delivery. In truth, many women have low-pitched speaking voices and men can have quite high-pitched speaking voices. Rather than looking at pitch, perhaps it is better to focus on delivery. Sometimes a breathier speaking voice is effective for feminizing a voice, and Dr. R.T. Sataloff also recommends becoming aware of how you speak: "Shall we go to dinner?" instead of, "Let's go to dinner!".

Adding estrogen to the body will not raise the pitch of a voice, but the sudden stopping of estrogen certainly has a dramatic impact. There is a lot of information throughout this book on the effects of menopause because it is such a huge transition for female bodies. There are estrogen receptors on the vocal folds, and as you will read in the chapters, "The menopausal voice – singing through the storm" by Barbara Fox DeMaio, PhD, and "Aging, HRT, and stabilizing the voice" by Lisa Popeil, menopause can wreak havoc on the female voice. So, what is to be done?

The effects of menopause is a theme that winds through all of the chapters, but that should not distract you from the wealth of information on aging voice that applies equally to everyone moving into their fifties, sixties and beyond. Just as regular exercise is recommended to keep your body stronger, singing is good exercise for all voices and one of the healthiest things you can do for your self, your body and your mind. There is a broad spectrum of information in the following chapters that will guide you in using your speaking and singing voice wisely, comfortably, and enjoyably, and instruct you in strengthening your voice and your breath so that you won't sound old.

3

The menopausal voice – singing through the storm

Barbara Fox DeMaio

What happens during menopause for the singer? It depends on a lot of factors, mostly involving hormones and also normal aging. Not all singers have the same experience; some singers lose range, others notice a change in vocal color and still others experience both. Singers who use "head-dominant" production (as in classical voice) are particularly vulnerable during menopause, as the first signs of vocal deterioration are often noted in high notes and pianissimos (Abitbol, 1999). These changes can also be distressing for singers who aren't professionals, but who do enjoy singing in choir and performing in community theatre.

For all women, admitting to menopausal symptoms brings up the topic of aging, and in the youth-oriented culture of today, aging in a taboo subject (Bernstein, 2005). Male singers can sing well into their 60's and beyond with very little change in the voice, but women start to experience changes as early as 35 or 40, depending on when menopause begins (Abitbol, 1999). Historically, menopause has been treated as a disease, rather than a natural part of the aging process. Feminist writings of the last 20 years have begun to attack the stigma attached to this time of life (McCrea and Markle, 1984), but despite recent research, over the years there has been an alarming amount of gender bias and misinformation both in research methods and the reporting of symptoms (Pinkerton and Zion, 2006).

During the time of the Greeks, 400 BC, women rarely lived past the age of 27, and menopause was uncommon. It is only since the 1800's that the life expectancy has increased to a point that menopause has become a regular part of the female experience. A young woman born in 1980 can expect to live to the age of 92; this means that a woman experiences menopause for about half of her lifetime (Abitbol,

2006). Now that women commonly experience menopause, scientists have begun to research the challenges that this transitional period brings and look for treatments for the symptoms.

The building blocks of the vocal mechanism

The voice consists of an energy source (the breath), a vibrator (the vocal folds) and a resonator (the vocal tract) (Doscher, 1994). The vocal folds reside in the larynx, which consists of the cricoid cartilage that sits on top of the trachea, the thyroid cartilage that is a shield-like cartilage that sits on top of the cricoid cartilage, the arytenoid cartilages that are located inside of the thyroid cartilage, the hyoid bone and the epiglottis. This complex mechanism is in a constant state of change from birth to death. The hyoid bone starts to ossify (turn into bone) at the age of two, the cricoid and thyroid cartilages begin to ossify in the 20s, and the arytenoids cartilages ossify in the early 30s. Except for the cuneiform and corniculate cartilages on the thyroid cartilage, the entire laryngeal skeleton ossifies around the age of 65 in both men and women (Sataloff and Linville, 2006). Ossification may actually be beneficial to the larynx in the third decade. Ingo Titze, a leading voice scientist, speculates that this hardening of the laryngeal framework supports the tension of the vocal folds more efficiently than cartilage, since cartilage can deform under stress (Titze, 1992). This would explain why dramatic voices tend to mature later; the vocal folds of a dramatic voice need a sturdier framework in order to vibrate efficiently.

Hormones contribute to changes in the voices of both men and women throughout life. A child's voice is sexless; little boys and little girls are vocally indistinguishable. At puberty, sex hormones appear – estrogens and progesterone in girls, androgens in boys – and this triggers the development of the third layer of epithelium cells on the vocal folds. This final development of the striated muscle of the vocal folds helps a girl develop both higher and lower harmonics as she becomes a woman.

At five months, the ovary of the female fetus has 7 million follicles. At puberty, there are only 300,000 follicles. By forty there are only 25,000 follicles; by the time a woman is 55, none remain. This lack of follicles means a lack of progesterone (Abitbol, 2006). Without progesterone, and with decreasing levels of estrogen, the antagonist receptors of the female hormones on the vocal folds and elsewhere cease to function. They will be affected by the male/androgen hormones thanks to the sex hormone binding globulin, a small molecule that will bring androgen to all of the receptors (Abitbol, 1998).

In boys, puberty sends the androgen testosterone to the estrogen receptors of the vocal folds, helping the child's voice lower into adult range. Something similar happens to women during menopause, causing the lowering of the voice associated with menopause. Once androgen attaches to the estrogen receptors of the vocal folds, there is no going back; the lowering is permanent (Abitbol, 1998). The slight permanent lowering of the female voice that occurs during puberty is caused by the appearance of steroid hormones in the body; on days prior to menstruation, some women experience temporary vocal lowering, due to the delicate balance between estrogen and progesterone that are part of the normal menstrual cycle. This is a temporary condition and not related to the hormonal shifts that occur during menopause (Meurer, et al, 2004).

It is difficult to distinguish normal aging, presbylaryngis, from the effects of menopause. It occurs in both men and women, and the connection to hormonal changes is not clear.

Vocal aging

The aging process causes changes in the laryngeal cartilages and joints, the muscles of the inner parts of the larynx, the covering of the vocal fold (epithelium) and the way that the nerves "innervate" the larynx, telling the larynx what to do; these changes affect the voice. The elastic cartilages of the larynx, which include parts of the arytenoid cartilage, corniculate, and epiglottis, do not ossify during the normal ossification of the larynx discussed earlier. The hyaline cartilages (thyroid, cricoid, and most of the arytenoid) do, however, eventually ossify (Benninger and Thomas, 2006).

Joint surfaces also erode; the breakdown of collagen fiber in the cartilage and the irregular surfaces are all part of the age-related changes in the cricoarytenoid joint. The correct emission of tone that relies on the delicate balance formed by the arytenoids and the cricoid is jeopardized by this breakdown of the joint surface (Benninger and Thomas, 2006).

In addition to the ossification of the larynx, the muscles of the larynx weaken with time. Aging brings a loss of muscle fibers in both the thyroarytenoid muscle and the posterior cricoarytenoid muscle and a decrease in the number of neuromuscular junctions. Substantial age-related changes are also seen in the recurrent laryngeal nerve and the superior laryngeal nerve (Benninger and Thomas, 2006). These neuromuscular changes can disrupt the delicate balance of the larynx, resulting in the weakening of the muscle, leading to a reduction in strength, vocal fold bowing (where the vocal folds do not meet in the middle), and the loss of the ability to speak or sing

(Benninger and Thomas, 2006). Researchers continue to study what part of aging is caused by hormonal shifts in order to reduce the negative effects on the voice.

Menopausal symptoms

The most common negative symptoms of menopause include dryness of the throat, frequent throat clearing, a lowering of the pitch of the voice, and increased roughness and hoarseness in speaking and singing, as well as swelling in the vocal folds (Dhaeseleer, et al, 2011). Researchers differ on the percentage of women who will experience hot flashes or night sweats during the perimenopausal and menopausal years; some say 50% to 85%, and others 29% to 74%, depending on race (Archer, et al, 2011). Dryness is more common, is found in both men and women, and is not caused exclusively by hormonal issues, since the mucous glands dry up and reduce in number during normal aging of both sexes (Leden and Alessi, 1994). Emotional swings, on the other hand, although certainly made worse by the hormonal ups and downs of menopause (Drohan, 2004), could also be affected by a woman's emotional state at this important juncture in her life. Feminist authors such as Mary Crawford, who object to menopause being reduced to medical terms (Crawford, 2006), point out that the moods caused by stressful life events may be misattributed to menopause. Children grow up and leave the nest; partners die or leave; retirement or changes in employment are common during this period. A long history exists, especially in Western cultures, of psychiatric diagnoses such as "involutional melancholia" (depression) in menopausal women. African women have a more positive attitude toward menopause than their European counterparts, viewing it as a normal and unremarkable part of life; many African women cope with menopause with very little fuss and no paralyzing psychotic symptoms (Crawford, 2006).

Emotional aspects of menopause – menopause as a psychosis

In the 1800s, doctors believed that menopause was a nervous disorder that could easily lead to a range of physical and mental illnesses (Banks, 2002). In his 1857 treatise on the subject, Edmond Tilt referred to women in menopause as eccentric and unhinged. In the 19th century medical professionals continued to view menopause in a negative light (Tilt, 1857). What is now considered to be a normal part of aging was previously considered to be both a physical and mental illness, calling for bizarre treatments, ranging from mineral baths and sexual abstinence to bloodletting, opium use, and marijuana use. Researchers of that time thought that these problems were due to the presence of the ovaries, and sometimes suggested the removal of the ovaries in young women with nervous complaints (Banks, 2002).

Other perceptions of menopause

Even in today's society, we continue to value youth and beauty; a woman's value and status are dependent on her reproductive ability. Media images, even in magazines aimed at an older population, regularly use models under the age of 50 (Crawford, 2006). Stereotypes of grannies, witches, and the mother-in-law from hell are common. In a recent study, researchers concluded that Disney movies depict old women as ugly, evil, greedy, power hungry, and crazy (Crawford, 2006). In other words, aging itself is the culprit; youth is good, and age is bad and should be "cured" by the medical establishment.

When doctors prescribed estrogen to women who did not have any symptom other than normal aging, a practice popular in the 1960s, they were treating menopause as a disease. Robert Wilson, one of the main proponents of universal estrogen prescription, went so far as to call menopausal women a danger to society, calling them unstable and estrogen-starved (Banks, 2002). His treatment for this "dangerous condition" was hormone therapy, and in a series of both medical and popular articles and a 1966 book titled *Feminine Forever*, he proposed estrogen therapy as the key to the prevention and cure of the "disease" of menopause (Houck, 2006). In Dr. Wilson's opinion, estrogen replacement therapy should be used from birth onward to treat the deficiencies caused by menopause (Houck, 2006).

This type of attitude created a backlash in the women's movement. Good reasons for using hormone replacement exist, especially when dealing with the preservation of the aging voice. A woman's singing or speaking career can often be extended by the use of hormones, but due to the negative press of recent years, and the legitimate objection of the women's movement to treating normal aging as an enemy, some women will not seek out treatment even as their voices begin to fail. They listen to those who say that the problem is attitude, not hormones (Bloch, 2002). Treatments exist, however (including both hormones and vocal exercises), that can help women who use their voices in public speaking and singing.

Treatment options for menopausal symptoms affecting the voice

Hormone Replacement Therapy (HRT)

Estrogen replacement therapy (ERT) was popular in the 1960s, thanks to the work of Wilson and *Feminine Forever*, but in the 1970s concern about the connection between estrogen therapy and endometrial cancer caused a sharp drop in the number of prescriptions written (Houck, 2006). By the 1980s, the combination of progestin and estrogen was found to have a beneficial effect on osteoporosis and heart disease, but in the 1990s and into the 21st century new studies came out that caused doctors to warn that the dangers of ERT outweighed the benefits (Houck, 2006). After 1980, feminists began to oppose the routine prescription of replacement hormones due to the characterization of menopause as a disease; however, hormones were still prescribed in unprecedented numbers (Houck, 2006).

Despite the experience of elite singers and much anecdotal knowledge, it was not until the 1990s that Jean and Béatrice Abitbol began to look at the effect that menopause has on the voices of elite voice users. Abitbol, Abitbol, and Abitbol found hormone receptors on the vocal folds, establishing hormones as the cause of vocal changes in both men and women (Abitbol, Abitbol and Abitbol, 1999). Abitbol and his wife took smears of the vocal folds and the cervix and found that they are almost identical; the cells are the same (Abitbol, Abitbol and Abitbol, 1999). They also found that certain body types fare better than others during menopause. What Abitbol calls the "Rubens-type," a woman who resembles those in paintings by Peter Paul Rubens, has an advantage during menopause because the fat cells will metabolize the androgens ("male" hormones) to estrones ("female" hormones). When HRT is used in this type of patient, however, it must be more carefully controlled because the rate at which the fat cells will metabolize the androgens is not predictable. In the thinner, "Modigliani-type" woman, the impact of androgen will predominate, but HRT is easier to control. Abitbol found that the fluctuation of hormones during menopause causes edema (swelling) in the female vocal folds, affecting their vibration during several parts of the cycle, both with the loss of progesterone and the loss of estrogen. The glandular cells are above and under the vocal fold but not on the vocal fold itself so that its lubrication is from above and under. Reinke's edema (a swelling of the "Reinke" space in the top part of the vocal fold, also associated with smokers) is found in 95% of women who develop atrophy of the covering of the vocal folds (epithelium) and vocal fatigue caused by the lessening of oxygen to the vocal muscle (the thyroid arytenoid muscle) (Abitbol, 1998) .

Jean Abitbol firmly believes that HRT is necessary, even indispensable, in voice professionals in order to avoid the lowering of the voice and vocal aging (Abitbol, Abitbol and Abitbol, 1999). He also recommends including a regimen of multivitamin therapy such as magnesium, mineral salts, vitamins B_5, B_6, and E and venous tone stimulants such as troxerutine (Veinamitol) because this seemed clinically to improve tone, amplitude, and hydration of the vocal folds. This treatment has not been examined by other researchers, but Abitbol recommends that this therapy should be used as a treatment for menopausal vocal syndrome in professional voice users (Abitbol, Abitbol and Abitbol, 1999). At least one study followed women who had surgically induced menopause and found that those with surgically induced menopause who use hormone replacement therapy often find marked improvement in their voices, with the most improvement shown by those who use intranasal estrogen (Firat, et al., 2009). More research needs to be done to discover whether intranasal HRT is more efficient in all menopausal women. Some women, including celebrities like Oprah Winfrey and Suzanne Somers, have turned to bioidentical hormones in the belief that these hormones affect the body differently because they are made from plants and so perhaps will not be as damaging as traditional HRT. Leading experts, however, such as Isaac Schiff, chief of obstetrics and gynecology at Massachusetts General Hospital in Boston, tell patients that believing one type of estrogen is safer than another as far as breast cancer is concerned is just wishful thinking (Kotz, 2007).

McCrea and Markle, writing about the differences in the way that HRT is prescribed in the United States and the United Kingdom, points out that researchers in the United Kingdom have concentrated on the positive aspects of HRT, whereas researchers in the United States emphasize the negative aspects (McCrea and Markle, 1984). Despite this, British doctors prescribe HRT far less often than their American colleagues do. McCrea and Markle credit this difference to the way that the health systems are organized. The United Kingdom bases a doctor's income on the number of patients seen per year, not per visit, so therapies that do not require follow-up visits are preferred. American doctors work on a per-visit basis and are more likely to prescribe therapies that need close follow-up, such as HRT. They conclude that HRT therapy has more risks than benefits (McCrea and Markle, 1984).

Alternative treatment methods

Women suffering from hot flashes and insomnia and who are concerned about the increased incidents of breast cancer and heart disease associated with HRT often turn to natural remedies to avoid these risks. More than 12 clinical trials have been done on the safety of black cohosh, one of the most popular over-the-counter remedies. It can mimic some of the functions of HRT, and although it can cause mild gastrointestinal symptoms in some women it is generally well tolerated. Evening primrose oil helps hot flashes in some women but is not recommended for women with seizure disorders. In a 1999 American double-blind study published in the *Journal of Obstetrics and Gynecology*, researchers found that natural progesterone cream may reduce or completely eliminate hot flashes. Natural progesterone is usually made from wild yams or soy, but those creams available without a prescription are generally not effective. Any use of natural hormones should be carefully controlled by a homeopathic doctor who specializes in these types of treatments (Murray, 2001). Valerian root is an efficient herbal remedy for insomnia, and changes in diet such as the addition of phytoestrogens found in foods like soy, flaxseed, chickpeas, and vegetables like Brussels sprouts and broccoli that have been shown to have a mild effect mimicking estrogen or to modify estrogen metabolism (Edman and Rakel, 2012). Researcher, Heman-Ackah found that only 20% to 30% of menopausal women had symptoms that merited treatment with HRT and that the risks outweigh the benefits in most women. Dr. Heman-Ackah further states that even the professional voice user should weigh these risks carefully before considering HRT and also cautions against the use of soy and black cohosh herbal remedies (Heman-Ackah, 2004).

Barbara Doscher, whose book *The Functional Unity of the Singing Voice* is considered a classic in the voice pedagogy literature, offers practical advice for the aging voice. She suggests that it is equally important to maintain both a healthy vocal technique and the body in good physical condition. She writes that the deterioration of the voice can be avoided by following a healthy lifestyle and maintaining moderate weight, blood pressure, percentage of body fat, and vital breathing capacity (Doscher,1994). Abitbol, in his book *Odyssey of the Voice,* agreed (Abitbol, 2006).

Vocal regimens

The Ingo Titze straw exercise, readily available on YouTube, is just one of the many semi-occluded exercises (any exercise that partially closes that vocal tract between the lips and the top of the vocal folds, such as buzzing a straw, humming or open mouth "hung") that have been used with great success in voice therapy over the years. The Stemple vocal function exercises (which use a "buzz" at the mouth) and the Lessac-Madsen resonant voice training (which use "m" and "n") are also based on the same semi-occluded exercise principles. Titze explains why these regimens and other exercises such as lip buzzing and humming have worked well for singers for many years; simply stated, semi-occluded exercises change the way that the vocal folds vibrate. The vocal folds then vibrate in a more efficient, economic manner, which takes pressure off the instrument. (Titze, 2006). Semi-occluded exercise is an excellent vocal regimen for the aging voice (Sauder, 2010), where the thickening of the covering of the vocal folds can cause huskiness in the middle voice (Leden and Alessi, 1994).

Dolly Caywood Davis used two sets of vocal exercises with 21 women, ages 53 to 74, in an effort to improve vibrato rate. Group I was assigned the vocal function exercises by Joseph Stemple that were designed to improve the speaking voice. Group II was assigned a similarly designed set of standard singing exercises. In a four-week study, she found that all the participants improved their vibrato rate, with a slightly better result in the group using the Stemple exercises (Davis, 2000). Anecdotally, I have used the Stemple vocal function exercises when teaching menopausal woman as an efficient way of improving the quality and ease of the middle voice.

David L. Jones, a New York pedagogue for over 30 years, in his online article "Vocalizing through Menopause: Regaining Lost Vocal Function," has his own set of exercises to help singers dealing with the effects of menopause regain vocal function. Jones says that his exercises are an attempt to exercise the cricothyroid muscle and elicit the thinning of the vocalis muscle. He cites tongue tension as a problem in the menopausal voice, but it should be noted that tongue tension is a problem in voices of all ages and especially in English speakers. Although Jones instructs the singer to keep the jaw slightly down and back to assist the closing of the vocal folds, this type of movement is not advised by most other pedagogues (Jones, 2011). Doscher, for example, insists that the jaw must remain loose (Doscher, 1994).

Clearly, disagreement about pedagogical methods for the menopausal voice exists despite the growing body of research into the changes that menopause brings. I will now share some of the findings from my recent doctoral research that examined methods used by elite singers and voice teachers to cope with these changes.

Vocal changes attributable to menopause

Dryness was the vocal issue reported most often by the singers that I interviewed (seven out of thirteen); this particular symptom seems to be related to normal aging, because dryness is found in both men and women due to the atrophy of the mucous glands (Leden and Alessi, 1994). An unsteady vibrato or wobble can be found in the aging voices of both men and women, according to the literature; and are probably related to normal aging (Benninger and Murray, 2006). Interestingly, vibrato issues were reported by only two of the participants in my study; however, all the voice professionals except one mentioned it as an issue with their aging patients.

Vocal symptoms that are possibly influenced by hormone fluctuations include a loss of flexibility, passaggio issues, and loss of range. As at least one study found, singers in my study who reported use of HRT had fewer vocal changes than the singers who chose not to use hormone therapy (Abitbol, 1999). The participants in my research were balanced equally; six of the singers used HRT or bioidentical hormones at some time during menopause, and eight did not use hormones of any kind for various reasons. Four of the participants either used hormones themselves or stated that some type of hormone therapy was a part of the possible treatment regimen for their clients. One of the participants reported that she uses bioidentical hormones, and one singer and one voice professional recommended them as a better alternative to traditional HRT. However, research does not support this view (Kotz, 2007).

The singers who did not subscribe to hormone therapy or a homeopathic substitute reported loss of flexibility; four of the five voice professionals also discussed this symptom. The literature suggests that this symptom may be attributed to the hardening of the cartilage in the larynx mentioned earlier that accompanies normal aging (Kotz, 2007). It is interesting to note that, in my study, only the singers not on HRT reported problems with flexibility, suggesting that hormone fluctuations may be partially responsible for this symptom.

As was true with loss of vocal flexibility, I found in my study that only the singers who were not on HRT reported trouble with either the upper or lower passaggio. All the voice professionals in the study reported passaggio issues in their menopausal clients. Once again, although the literature suggests that changes in the larynx as a part of normal aging might be responsible, it is interesting to note that only the participants who were not on hormone therapy reported passaggio issues.

Few women in the study mentioned loss of high range as a symptom, a finding that is contradicted by research and this author's personal experience. This might be because the loss of high notes for any reason, illness, age, or menopause is a reason for concern in the elite voice, and my participants may have been reluctant to mention it (Luchsinger, 1965). The five participants who did report loss of high range did not use HRT, suggesting that, at least in my study, hormone fluctuations might be responsible. Only one singer (who was a Broadway coloratura) reported no loss of range despite her decision to avoid HRT. However, she reported using a homeopathic regimen meant to stimulate the production of estrogen in the liver.

None of my research before conducting these interviews indicated that menopause might cause loss of low notes, however, all of the classical mezzo-sopranos in my study indicated that they had experienced this symptom. For this reason, the connection to hormone fluctuations is not clear; but I suspect that it is caused by the strengthening of the lower range, or chest voice, that causes an imbalance in the "vocal mix" that classical mezzos use in their chest voice. All of the operatic sopranos reported strengthening of low notes, including the participant who uses bioidentical hormones. Interestingly, one of the singers interviewed believed the change in her range might be due to teaching and not hormonal changes.

There is a lack of agreement among physicians and voice scientists about the use of hormone therapy (Abitbol, 1999; Sataloff 1991; Benninger, 2006; Heman-Ackah, 2004). and there was a similar lack of agreement among my participants. Of course, a small study like mine cannot establish the necessity of HRT for preserving vocal range, however, singers in the study who used HRT had fewer vocal problems than the singers who chose not to use hormones. Hormonal treatments are not possible, or desirable, for every professional singer; however, researchers such as Abitbol, Sataloff, and Benninger suggest that this therapy can be an important part of preserving the aging female voice.

Physical changes attributable to menopause

The research that I read before my interviews (Sataloff, 2006, Benninger, 2006; Heman-Ackah, 2004) led me to believe that most of the participants would tell me that they had left their careers during or after menopause due to both physical and vocal changes. However, not a single participant reported that she ended her career as the result of menopause. Most of the singers involved were still singing at the time they were interviewed, although not as frequently. The singers who have continued to perform have changed their repertoire, mostly due to appearance and stamina, and many reported that they had begun to teach as well as perform. One participant left her career earlier than most singers in this study for both medical reasons and a desire to spend more time with her daughter as she was growing up. Another of the participants would be happy to sing more than she does now, but said, "There is a stigma right now about age, I tell you. I'm hardly singing at all, and the only thing I can think is age, though I'm still able to sing great." As Tamara Bernstein argued in the Classical Singer article mentioned earlier, the perception that women have shorter careers in opera and musical theater than men is commonly held. The women that I interviewed are pushing back against this perception; according to them, shorter careers are a result of growing older in a profession that values youth and beauty.

Not surprisingly, then, the most common advice given by the participants was a healthy diet and exercise as well as good vocal hygiene. This was also the advice of researchers such as Abitbol, Sataloff, Benninger, and others.

Two of the participants urged singers to be more supportive of each other when going through the menopausal transition. Women are reluctant to share their aging experience with others; the images that women see in their daily lives can be devaluing and shaming, based on the loss of fertility and physical attractiveness (Ambler Walter, 2000). One singer said, "[The aging experience] is probably less of an issue now than it might have been in the past, but I think that … it's grieving to a certain extent, if you have to go through putting away a certain beloved role … [you must] really offer encouragement [to yourself] in all the things that you are now." She also emphasized that singers need to be supportive of one another when a change of repertoire is necessary, stressing the need to "keep expanding your horizons because there is just an endless amount of repertoire." Two of the voice professionals interviewed stated that the most helpful coping strategy of all is for women to surround themselves with a supporting community of friends, a trusted voice teacher or coach, and a physician as they negotiate this change in their lives. As one of them put it: "Even opening the door to look at these issues seriously, and take them seriously, and even to not make them, quote, 'women's issues,' but 'being's issues,' so that it takes them out of the realm of, 'oh, that's just a woman's problem,' is huge."

Emotional issues identified in my study

Five of the singers interviewed reported emotional issues, some more severe than others, and two of the Voice Professionals spoke to the problem, as well. The participant that spoke the longest about her emotional issues with menopause and aging said; "it seemed to me that just the whole act of singing, and I don't know if this is connected to menopause or if it's psychological, just became more difficult. You know, just getting out there and going to sing." She went on to say that the changes caused her to lose her ease in singing, and "then the act of singing became a frightening thing." She felt that part of the problem was that she did not have someone to talk to about the issue –

> And the thing is … when you're going through this, who do you talk to? Because this has nothing to do with menopause, but who do you talk to, because any sense or feeling of weakness that is perceived in you, and it's a very funny thing, but people go on the attack. Or at least I've found that to be so, so you suffer privately. And … the teacher that I was studying with before … said, I didn't have any problem with menopause. And I asked one of her friends and she said, yes, she didn't have any problems whatsoever. Because I needed to understand … I would say that it was the instability of the lower voice, because it wasn't that I was afraid, like stage fright, what made me afraid was that I did not know what my voice was going to

do. Whereas all my life, since I was a child, the one thing that I knew that I could do, regardless of what people said about me, I got teased a lot because I was a fat kid … I knew that I could sing. And so here, all of a sudden, because of these physical changes, I can sing but not like I used to. And so, the other effect of it is the loss of confidence. And that, I think, is more devastating than just going through the physical changes … Every day I wake up and I thank God that I can still sing, because honestly it scares me to think … I'm not going to sing anymore"

One singer that I interviewed felt that menopause caused her to lose her passion and enthusiasm which also affected her voice; "you have to keep your curiosity and keep your enthusiasm, which I found was extremely difficult, to keep my enthusiasm during menopause … I remember saying I've lost my passion, I want my passion back. Just my passion for living, for everything … and that of course affects the voice." Another singer spoke to the emotion of leaving a role behind; "When you're not that anymore, you're not going to put that costume on again, what does that mean?" Yet another found that the peri-menopausal period was much more difficult emotionally and feels that led to weight gain. Another singer also had emotional problems during peri-menopause but feels that the nutritional regimen that she now follows has helped her immensely. A type of dark humor sometimes showed up in the interviews; one singer joked "I take anti-depressants, so that could mask any other craziness that's going on." One SVS said that when a client does end a career after the aging/menopausal changes, she is "not sure it's so much the voice change as the emotional impact that the voice change has." One of the most heartbreaking stories came from an SVS who had a client who could not get past the changes in her voice, and no longer sings at all. She realizes that –

> "When the voice starts going kerflooey, there's an emotional component just in that that's very, very powerful. But this was not that, this was an additional something spinning on top of it. And, I really thought that that made the kind of progress that some of the other people that I had, that had kind of gotten back on their vocal feet, and kind of found a way to keep going, was not happening with this other person. She just, almost needed, to have some medical reason why she couldn't function, and she was more interested in having an excuse about why it was bad then in having a reason to make it work even though it was bad."

So how do those that continue to sing get past these emotional changes? What helps them find their way? This was one of my favorite statements; "You feel like a woman with no feet if you can't sing, it's something that's taken away that is so, so much a part of you … And other than severe illness, I can't see why that is not possible for every woman at every age. I mean, you'd have to convince me that we have to suddenly become mute"

Pedagogical strategies for the menopausal voice

My initial interest in this project resulted from my own experience singing through menopause, and a lack of literature with pedagogical strategies for the menopausal voice. Although there was very little agreement among the women in my study about what caused vocal changes during menopause, the vocalises they suggested were similar to each other. One recommended one-note warm-up exercises that were very similar to the Stemple vocal function exercises (Sauder, et al., 2010), mentioned earlier, recommended by one of the Singing Voice Specialists (SVS) interviewed. Arpeggios and onset exercises were identified in the literature and also recommended by all of the voice professionals. Stretching into both head and chest every day and warming the middle voice slowly were found in the literature and echoed by nine study participants. Singing repertoire every day, although not found in the literature, was strongly recommended by two of the three SVSs in the study. In short, these women all felt that singing was a "use it or lose it" proposition.

Early pedagogical texts such as those by Nicola Vaccaj and Giovanni Battista Lamperti use small intervals expanding to octave slides to unify the voice and work through the passaggios of the voice. All three of the SVSs, however, suggested adding semi-occluded straws, lip trills, or lip buzzing to this interval work in order to add to their efficiency as treatments for passaggio issues. As one SVS explained, "I'll … have them do a lot of pivot work [half steps back and forth] on their semi-occluded sounds." One unexpected recommendation came from another SVS: although the literature (and most pedagogical texts) recommended increased breath management to help with passaggio issues, this SVS recommended the following –

> I try to help the singer find where the change point now is, and one of the ways of getting through, especially that lower passaggio change, is to take some of the pressure off the voice, in other words, go through it with less volume, while you're in the actual transition from a stronger head mix to a stronger chest mix, right at the point of change, to take some breath pressure off of that moment.

This SVS also disagreed with traditional vocal pedagogues who "would try to stabilize [or lock down] a larynx in a woman that had not an aging issue but a vocal fold weakness issue [because that can give] some stability, but it [is] not a very pretty sound."

Although I began with the assumption that everyone I interviewed would be completely unique, I was surprised by just how unique the participants were. I did not expect to hear that at least one singer did not warm up during her career, and others who, even though they still sing professionally, do not use their voices every day unless preparing for a role. One surprising result was the singer who reported that she is losing her sense of perfect pitch as she ages; I have since found that research exists on this phenomenon, although I did not identify it in my initial research. Finally, because they are such a common symptom of menopause, (Crawford, 2006, Archer, 2011) it was interesting to hear that only four of the singers interviewed had hot flashes and only one of the singers said that her hot flashes were severe.

Conclusion

My study was designed to listen to the voices of these professionals, as their journey can be a guide for all female singers as they approach menopause. Interestingly, the experiences of the women I interviewed are remarkably similar and suggest that most singers will experience changes in range, flexibility, and stamina as they age.

Although there is disagreement about the use of HRT by menopausal and post-menopausal singers, the singers that I interviewed who used HRT or a bio-identical substitute reported little or no change to their singing voice after menopause. This finding suggests that the use of HRT could be considered a quality of life issue for elite singers.

The vocal exercises identified have already proven their value in my voice studio as I work with menopausal singers. I am grateful to the women who shared their experiences with me, and I look forward to continuing this research in an attempt to dispel the perception that women must have shorter careers than men.

Exercises from this author's studio

Head Voice Exercises

Middle Voice Exercises

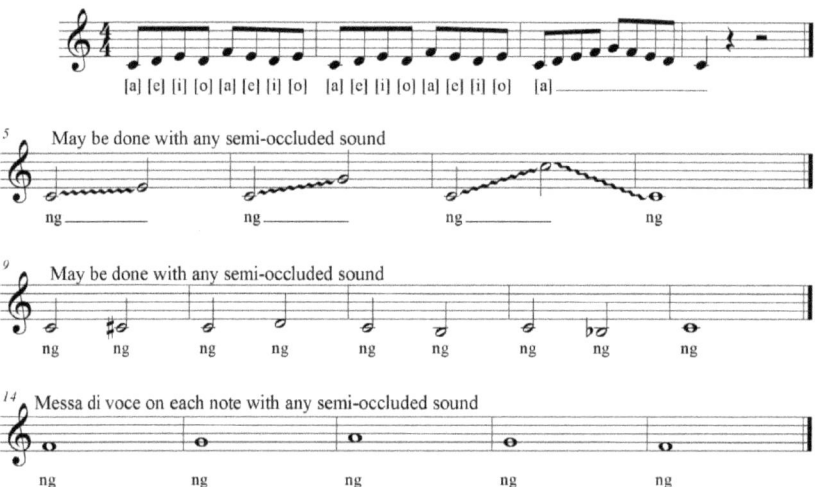

Bibliography

Abitbol, Jean (1998) The Diva Twilight; Female Voice at Menopause. Paper presented at the 45th National Association of Teachers of Singing Convention, Toronto, July 3–7, 2 Cassette tapes.

Abitbol, Jean (2006) *Odyssey of the Voice*. Translated by Patricia Crossley. San Diego, CA: Plural Publishing, Inc.

Abitbol, Jean, Patrick Abitbol and Béatrice Abitbol (1999) Sex Hormones and the Female Voice *Journal of Voice* 13(3): 424–446.

Ambler Walter, Carolyn (2000) The Psychosocial Meaning of Menopause: Women's Experiences *Journal of Women & Aging* 12(3/4): 117–131.

An Xue, Steve and Jianping Hao, Grace (2003) Changes in the Human Vocal Tract Due to Aging and the Acoustic Correlates of Speech Production: A Pilot Study *Journal of Speech, Language and Hearing Research* 46: 689–701.

An Xue, Steve and Deliyski, Dimitar (2001) Effects of Aging on Selected Acoustic Voice Parameters: Preliminary Normative Data and Educational Implications *Educational Gerontology* 27: 159–168.

Archer, D.F., W. Sturdee, R. Baber, *et al*. (2011) Menopausal Hot Flushes and Night Sweats: Where are we now? *Climacteric* 14: 515–528.

Avery-Hill, Laura K. (2004) Pregnancy and the Voice. DMA diss., Faculty of the Department of Music, University of Houston.

Awan, Shaween N. (2006) The aging female voice: Acoustic and respiratory data *Clinical Linguistics & Phonetics* 20: 171–180.

Banks, Emily (2002) From Dogs' Testicles to Mares' Urine: The Origins and Contemporary Use of Hormonal Therapy for the Menopause *Feminist Review* 72: 2–25.

Benninger, Michael and Murray, Thomas, eds. (2006) *The Performer's Voice*. San Diego, CA: Plural Publishing, Inc.

Bernstein, Tamara (2005) Is the opera house hot or is it just me? (effects of menopause on the voice) *Classical Singer* March 18: 26–29.

Bloch, A. (2002) Self-awareness during the menopause *Maturitas* 41: 61–68.

Bone, Amber Sudduth (2011) Time Use, Strategic Behaviors, Technical Content, and Cognitive and Motivational Profiles in Collegiate Vocal Music Practice. DMA diss., University of Washington.

Boulet, Monique J. and Björn J. Oddens (1996) Female Voice Changes Around and After the Menopause – an Initial Investigation *Maturitas* 23: 15–21.

C. Bohr, *et al*. (2012) Correlation between coping strategies and subjective assessment of the voice-related quality of life of patients after resection of T1 and T2 laryngeal tumours. *European Archives Of Oto-Rhino-Laryngology* 269(9): 2091–2096.

Chae, Sung Won, Geon Choi, Hee Joon Kang, *et al*. (2001) Clinical Analysis of Voice Change as a Parameter of Premenstrual Syndrome *Journal of Voice* 15(2): 278–283.

Comins, Jayne (2003) Women with attitude: singing through the menopause *The Singer*, June/July: 24–25.

Crawford, Mary (2006) *Transformations; Women, Gender and Psychology*. New York, NY: McGraw-Hill.

Davis, Dolly Caywood (2000) A Study of the Effects of Two Kinds of Vocal Exercises on Selected Parameters in the Singing Voices of Women Over Age Fifty. Ph.D diss., Graduate College of The University of Iowa.

DeSoto, M. Catherine (2003) Drops in estrogen levels affect brain, body and behavior: reported relationship between attitudes and menopausal symptoms *Maturitas* **45**: 299–301.

D'haeseleer, Evelien, Herman Depypere, Sofie Claeys, and Kristiane Van Lierde (2012) The impact of menopause and hormone therapy on nasal resonance *Logopedics Phoniatrics Vocology* **37**: 69–74.

D'haeseleer, Evelien, Herman Depypere, Sofie Claeys, *et al.* (2011) The impact of menopause on vocal quality *Menopause: The Journal of The North American Menopause Society* **18**(3): 267–272.

D'haeseleer, Evelien, Herman Depypere, Sofie Claeys, *et al.* (2009) The Menopause and the Female Larynx, Clinical Aspects and Therapeutic Options: A Literature Review *Maturitas* **64**: 27–32.

Doscher, Barbara M. (1994) *The Functional Unity of the Singing Voice*, 2ed., Lanham, MD: The Scarecrow Press, Inc.

Drohan, Marie Antoinette (2004) The Effect on the Singing Voice and the Vocal Longevity of Professional Singers. Ed.D diss., Teachers College, Columbia University.

Edman, Joel S., Kondrad, Lauren B., Rakel, Birgit (2012) The Use of Nutrition and Integrative Medicine or Complementary and Alternative Medicine (CAM) for Singers, Part 2 *Journal of Singing* **68**(3): 291–297.

Edwin, Robert (2012) Voice Pedagogy for Aging Singers (Including the Author) *Journal of Singing* **68**(5): 561–563.

F.I.C.R.S. de Jong, *et al.* (2010) Biopsychosocial Impact of Voicing and General Coping Style in Teachers. *Folia Phoniatrica Et Logopaedica* **62**(1/2): 40–46.

Firat, Yezdan, Yaprak Engin-Ustun, Ahmet Kizilay, *et al.* (2009) Effect of Intranasal Estrogen on Vocal Quality *Journal of Voice* **23**(6): 716–720.

Fleming-DeBerger, Rachelle (2011) Guidelines and criteria to assess singing and music training in baccalaureate music theater programs. DMA diss., University of Miami.

Fox DeMaio, Barbara (2013) The Effect of Menopause on the Elite Singing Voice – Singing Through the Storm. DMA diss., Shenandoah University. (not yet published)

Gregory, Naomi D., Chandran, Swapna, Lurie, Deborah and Sataloff, Robert T. (2012) Voice Disorders in the Elderly *Journal of Voice* **26**(2): 254–258.

Haumschild, Mary S., Haumschild, Ryan J. (2010) Postmenopausal females and the link between oral bisphosphonates and osteonecrosis of the jaw: A clinical review *Journal of the American Academy of Nurse Practitioners* **22**: 534–539.

Heman-Ackah, Yolanda D. (2004) Hormone Replacement Therapy: Implications of the Women's Health Initiative for the Perimenopausal Singer *Journal of Singing*, **60**, (5): 471–475.

Houck, Judith A. (2006) *Hot and Bothered; Women, Medicine and Menopause in Modern America*. Cambridge, MA: Harvard University Press.

Jones, David L. (2011) Vocalizing Through Menopause: Regaining Lost Vocal Function. http://www.voiceteacher.com/menopause.html (accessed April 27, 10:51 pm.)

Kotz, Deborah (2007) Bioidentical Hormones: Safer For Hot Flashes than HRT? *US News and World Reports* (Oct.18) http://health.usnews.com/healthnews/familyhealth/articles/2007/10/18/hrt-dilemma (accessed October 21, 2012).

Laureano, Janaína Mendes, Marcos Felipe S. Sá, Rui A. Ferriani and Gustavo S. Romao (2009) Variations of Jitter and Shimmer Among Women In Menacme and Postmenopausal Women *Journal of Voice* 23(6): 687–689.

Leden, Hans von and Alessi, David M. (1994) The Aging Voice, in *Vocal Arts Medicine: The Care and Prevention of Professional Voice Disorders*, edited by Benninger, Michael, Jacobson, Barbara, Johnson, Alex. New York, NY: Thieme Medical Publishers, Inc.

Liu, Peng, Chen, Zhaocong, Jones, Jeffery A., et al. (2011) Auditory Feedback Control of Vocal Pitch during Sustained Vocalization: A Cross-Sectional Study of Adult Aging *PLOS ONE* 6(7) http://www.plosone.org/article/info%3Adoi%2F10.1371%2Fjournal.pone.0022791 (accessed September 23, 2012).

Luchsinger, Richard, Godfrey E. Arnold (1965) *Voice-Speech-Language, Clinical Communicology: Its Physiology and Pathology* Belmont, CA: Wadsworth.

Maines, Sarah (2012) The Efficacy of Vocal Function Exercises in the Practice Regimen of Undergraduate Music Theatre Majors. DMA diss., Shenandoah University. (not yet published)

Marnocha, Suzanne K., Bergstrom, Marshelle, Dempsey, Leona F. (2011) The lived experience of perimenopause and menopause *Contemporary Nurse* 37(2): 229–240.

McCoy, Scott (2006) *Your Voice: An Inside View.* Princeton, NJ: Inside View Press.

McCrea, Frances B., Gerald E. Markle (1984) The Estrogen Replacement Controversy in the USA and UK: Different Answers to the Same Question? *Social Studies of Science* 14 (1): 1–26.

Meurer, Eliséa Maria, Maria Celeste Osório Wender, Helena von Eye Corleta and Edison Capp (2004) Phono-articulatory Variations of Women in Reproductive Age and Postmenopausal *Journal of Voice* 18(3): 369–374.

Murray, Jenni (2001) *Is it me, or is it hot in here? A modern woman's guide to the menopause.* London: Vermilion.

Nauraine, Annette (2009) Singers and the Afterlife: What It's Like After a Singing Career *Classical Singer*, December. http://www.classicalsinger.com/magazine/article.php?id=2021 (accessed February 11, 2013).

Nishio, Masaki, Tanaka, Yasuhiro, Niimi, Seiji (2011) Analysis of Age-Related Changes in the Acoustic Characteristics of Voices *Journal of Communications Research* 2(1): 65–77.

Oyarzún, Patricia, Sepúlveda, Alfredo, Valdivia, Maria, et al. (2011) Variations of the Vocal Fold Epithelium in a Menopause Induced Model *International Journal of Morphology* 29(2): 377–381.

Pinkerton, Joann V., Zion, Adrienne S. (2006) Vasomotor Symptoms in Menopause: Where We've Been and Where We're Going *Journal of Women's Health* 15(2): 135–145.

Prakup, Barbara L. (2009) Acoustic Measures of the Voices of Older Singers and Non-Singers. Ph.D diss., Kent State University College of Education, Health and Human Services.

Price, Kathy Kessler (2010) Acoustic and Perceptual Assessments of Experienced Adult Female Singers According to Menopausal Status, Hormone Replacement Therapies, Singing Experience, and Preferred Singing Mode. Ph.D diss., University of Kansas.

Raj, Anoop, Bulbul Gupta, Anidita Chowdhury and Shelly Chadha (2010) A Study of Voice Changes In Various Phases of Menstrual Cycle and in Postmenopausal Women *Journal of Voice* 24(3): 363–368.

Reeves, Keith O. (2005) Hormone Therapy for the Female Performing Artist *Medical Problems of Performing Artists* 20(1): 48–51. *Music Index*, EBSCO*host* (accessed September 23, 2012).

Sapienza, CM, and J Dutka (1996) Glottal Airflow Characteristics of Women's Voice Production Along an Aging Continuum *Journal of Speech & Hearing Research* 39(2): 322–328. *CINAHL with Full Text*. Web. 16 September.

Sataloff, Robert Thayer and Linville, Sue Ellen (2006) The Effects of Age on the Voice in Vol. II of *Vocal Health and Pedagogy: Advanced Assessment and Treatment*, 2ed., Edited by Sataloff, Robert T. San Diego, CA: Plural Publishing, Inc.

Sataloff, Robert Thayer, Spiegel, Joseph R. and Caputo Rosen, Deborah (1991) The Effects of Age on the Voice, in *Professional Voice: The Science and Art of Clinical Care*, Edited by Sataloff, Robert T. New York, NY: Raven Press.

Sataloff, Robert Thayer (1996) The Effects of Menopause on the Singing Voice *Journal of Singing* 54(2): 39–42.

Sauder, Cara, Roy, Nelson, Roy, Tanner, *et al.* (2010) Vocal Function Exercises for Presbylaryngis: A Multidimensional Assessment of Treatment Outcomes *Annals of Otology, Rhinology and Laryngology* 119(7): 460–467.

Siarris, Catherine Froneberger (2009) The Aging Female Voice: Medical Treatments and Pedagogical Techniques for Combatting the Effects of Aging with Emphasis on Menopause. DMA diss., University of South Carolina, 2009.

Tilt, E.J. (1857) *Change of Life in Health and Disease*. London: Churchill.

Titze, Ingo R. (1992) *Principles of Voice Production*. New York, NY: Prentice Hall.

Titze, Ingo R. (2006) Voice Training and Therapy with a Semi-Occluded Vocal Tract: Rationale and Scientific Underpinnings *Journal of Speech, Language and Hearing Research* 49(April): 448–459.

Vlasiadis, Konstantinos Z., Damilakis, John, Velegrakis, George, *et al.* (2008) Relationship between BMD, dental panoramic radiographic findings and biochemical markers of bone turnover in diagnosis of osteoporosis *Maturitas* 59: 226–233.

Wadsworth, Gill (2000) Hearing Midlife Voices: Assessing Different Methods for Researching Women's Experiences of Menopause and Midlife *Women's Studies International Forum* 23(5): 645–654.

Woodward, Kathleen (2005) Performing Age, Performing Gender: The Legacy of Carolyn Heilbrun *Tulsa Studies in Women's Literature* 24(2): 283–290.

Wu, Kwok H., Tobias, Martha L. Tobias, Kelley, Darcy B., (2003). Estrogen Receptor Expression in Laryngeal Muscle in Relation to Estrogen-Dependent Increases in Synapse Strength *Neuroendocrinology* 78: 72–80.

Yang, Cheng-Chieh, Chung, Yuh-Mei, Chi, Lin-Yang, *et al.* (2011) Analysis of Verbal Diadochokinesis in Normal Speech Using the Diadochokinetic Rate Analysis Program *Journal of Dental Sciences* 6(4): 221–226.

Zöllner, Y.F., C. Acquadro, M. Schaefer (2005) Literature Review of Instruments to Assess Health-Related Quality of Life During and After Menopause *Quality of Life Research* 14(2): 309–327.

4

Options and pesky side effects

Martha Howe

The following are a few topics of interest for the fifth decade onward. This is not a list of specific medications, as that would be too much of a moving target and outside the scope of this book. Know that most prescriptions have a drying effect on the voice, which just adds to the drying effects of aging itself. Polypharmacy can be a problem, when each specialist gives us medication and no one is 'quarterbacking' all of the interactions. It is good to look over your medications and eliminate what you don't really need, or what you no longer need. Be sure and talk with your physician and/or your pharmacist about possible interactions between your various medications.

Above all, read the paperwork that comes with those medications for side effects and interactions, paying attention to key words like hoarseness, joint stiffness, balance, dry-mouth, cough, heartburn, blood-thinners, androgens, or generalized terms that imply those properties, effects, and symptoms. Sometimes you need to search online on a reputable medical site for a more comprehensive list of side effects. There is a list of how various medications affect your voice on the National Center for Voice & Speech (NCVS) web site. Go to ncvs.org/rx.html or to ncvs.org and enter rx in the search function. The list was created by the voice scientists at NCVS with input from an experienced pharmacist and you can search this list by brand or generic names, drug groups, manufacturer, scientific herb names, and symptoms. Be sure to ask questions of your physician and pay close attention to what's going on in your body with the various medications.

Also pay attention to the ingredients in items from the homeopathic and herbal shelves. Do not assume that homeopathic and herbal remedies should be automatically trusted or that they are risk-free. I use them all the time, but carefully and mindfully. It is your body, do your homework, always keep your physician in the loop, and don't try anything new (addition or subtraction) shortly before a performance. That is not the time to add the stress of the unexpected and unknown!

Aspirin, blood thinners and the NSAIDs

Be careful using these when using your voice. People take aspirin and nonsteroidal anti-inflammatory drugs (NSAIDs), like Advil and Motrin, for pain and to reduce inflammation. But there can be problems if you are about to deliver a strong, emphatic speech or sing for a length of time, as they also prevent clotting of the blood and promote bleeding. So if your throat/vocal folds are irritated and you are pushing your voice, you run the risk of doing damage to your vocal folds with vocal hemorrhaging as a worst-case scenario. I have been there when a young tenor walked off stage spitting blood. We covered him in platitudes and 'all will be wells', but his career ended that evening.

The good news is that with older voices, the vocal-shearing forces (the collision forces of the vocal folds striking each other to make sound) tend to be lower because of the loss of muscle mass and strength. Because the vocal folds don't slam into each other with as much force, older singers don't tend to suffer from nodules and polyps. If you have a history of vocal fold hemorrhage, then you need to be careful with blood thinners but otherwise, don't be afraid to use them when they are needed for your overall health.

It is not unusual to take aspirin or an NSAID before bed to help the voice or your body recover from a long, tiring day. Please make sure they NEVER hit an empty stomach and be sure and stay upright for TWENTY MINUTES after taking pills. Whatever you do, do not just swallow them dry. I've spoken with someone in her twenties recovering from a severely damaged esophagus; She took aspirin and fell right asleep. Eating, speaking, and swallowing were all difficult and painful for her as she was healing.

Asthma inhalers

There is not much research yet, but the steroids in them can cause problems. The older medications, where the steroids sat on the vocal folds, were damaging and thought to cause vocal fold atrophy. Now the steroids are delivered in smaller particles that travel more directly to the lungs. No atrophy has been seen yet from the non-steroidal inhalers.

Fungal laryngitis is a risk from the steroids in the inhalers. Dry particle inhalers can dry and irritate the vocal folds

Cortisone shots

Shots of corticosteroids are often given for knee and other joint pain. Recent studies bring into question whether they are harmful in the long run as they speed up the damage to the cartilage. Back in the 1970s, I had a bout of laryngitis during a performance run and was given cortisone to see me through. It was surreal, as I felt no pain and my voice worked fairly well, although I knew it was smoke and mirrors. Luckily it was a small role, I was young, and didn't incur lasting vocal damage.

Weigh the danger carefully, and if you must take a steroid, take them by mouth, NEVER use an inhaler.

Another possible side effect from corticosteroids, especially larger shots for knees and such, is that they can jolt a post-menopausal body into a full menstrual cycle. This can come as quite a shock to the unsuspecting. They can also launch adult-onset diabetes. Be careful.

CPAP machines

Continuous Positive Airway Pressure therapy (CPAP) is for those with obstructive sleep apnea. A CPAP machine increases the air pressure in the throat to keep the airway from collapsing during the in-breath. However, dryness can be an issue as the increased air pressure and airflow can be drying. Many people wear the mask over their mouths, which means you don't have the benefit of nasal hydration from breathing through your nose.

There are no studies yet of the various CPAPs' effect on the voice, but many people swear by how much better their voice sounds and works after starting to use one. Perhaps it is the oxygen, perhaps it is the better night's sleep, perhaps not having the pressure on the larynx of snoring, perhaps it is any, or all of the above. Just be mindful and take appropriate care of the mask so it doesn't become a health risk.

Type 1 and Type 2 Diabetes Mellitus

Common vocal symptoms are hoarseness and vocal straining, especially when blood glucose levels are swinging around. Add to this that hoarseness is a side-effect of several of the medications, along with brain fog, trouble concentrating, balance issues, stiff joints and upper respiratory infections, and clearly diabetes is not a professional voice user's friend. High blood glucose levels or spikes can make the voice feel unwieldy and rough. The voice feels much more normal and easy at lower blood glucose levels, but a long rehearsal or a performance can cause blood glucose to drop suddenly. Even an energetic singalong can cause a blood glucose drop. So, keep track of your carbohydrates to avoid spiking up, and pay attention to your readings to fend off sudden dips in your glucose, keeping apple juice or glucose tablets close to hand should you need them.

Dryness and clearing of the throat

As we age, the salivary glands slow down – especially those right below the vocal folds. This seems to be very bad planning, as the vocal folds are already drying out because the supply of estrogen has stopped to the vocal folds' estrogen receptors. Less saliva means not only a dryer larynx and throat, it also means the mucus that is always there as a necessary lubricant thickens up and becomes singularly unhelpful.

Drinking water will help overall body hydration, but of course does not directly affect the vocal folds (unless you've just swallowed 'the wrong way' and are busy coughing the water away from the folds).

Steam inhalation does get the moisture to the larynx and vocal folds, but again, be very careful. It is possible to burn those delicate tissues if the steam is too condensed; don't inhale the steam from the spout of the kettle, open the lid or use a pan, and pay attention to what you feel. It is also questionable how helpful it will be the more time there is between steaming and speaking or singing, although it will help loosen up the mucus.

Guaifenesin is very good for thinning mucus. It is found in many cold medications but just be careful to check what else is in the pill so you don't add a decongestant or other drying agent to the mix.

Menopause, estrogen, androgens, and HRT

Each woman's experience of menopause is unique. Some women sail through easily and for some it is dramatically difficult. The effect on the voice is individual and somewhat dependent on genetics, vocal technique, health and type of workload.

Do not assume that your primary physician is up to speed on the best treatments for menopause. In the August/September 2018 issue of *AARP The Magazine*, an article by Jennifer Wolff, 'What doctors don't know about menopause may harm you', presented some startling statistics. Evidently, menopause is not being taught at most medical schools and a recent survey showed that it was taught in only 20% of the ob-gyn residency programs. Thus, close to 20% of medical residents are 'barely comfortable' discussing or treating menopause. Yet close to one-third of the women in the U.S. are post-menopausal and, not surprisingly, of the sixty percent that seek medical attention, nearly three-quarters are left untreated. Managing menopause involves more time spent talking with a patient, is not as lucrative, and requires an extensive understanding of the effects on every system in the body of the loss of estrogen.

Hormone Replacement Therapy (HRT) and bioidentical hormone therapy

Barbara Fox DeMaio's chapter in this book, 'Singing through the storm', gives an excellent overview of research through 2017 on the benefits and issues around HRT, along with what is known about bioidentical hormones. As of this publication, there have been limited rigorous studies on bioidenticals, and most of the information is from individual experience and perception. Look closely at the ingredients in homeopathic remedies, as they can include testosterone or other androgens, whose permanent effects are discussed in this book..

Estrogen

There is no easy answer here. Without supplemental estrogen, the voice's high range will probably suffer so it is a career decision for coloraturas and all mid-career sopranos and high mezzos. Each body is different and will react to the changes in natural estrogen levels differently. There is also family history and overall health to take into consideration, as the possible side-effects of both estrogen loss and hormone replacement therapies are dramatic.

In 2002, the National Institutes of Health (NIH) added estrogen to its list of known human carcinogens (Report on Carcinogens, December 11, 2002) after the highly publicized clinical trials in the 1990s on the effects of hormone therapy on healthy menopausal women. This study was stopped early because the women taking estrogen plus progestin experienced higher than expected rates of blood clots, heart attacks, strokes and breast cancer. Plus, women over 65 taking estrogen and progesterone had twice the rate of dementia. Because of these findings, the levels of hormones in hormone replacement therapies have been changed and lowered. To confuse the issue, there are more recent studies with different levels that produced different conclusions. There is a great deal not known yet. It is your body, your options, your choice. Do your research.

Testosterone and other androgens: your escalator to the basement

Sometimes androgens are given to women to treat endometriosis. They are also prescribed when women feel they don't have enough energy or seek a boost in their libido. Take them only if you really love being an alto. You could lose a third off the top of your range before you even notice there's a problem. When a woman takes testosterone as a supplement or a gel (or comes into contact with a partner's testosterone gel), it changes the larynx just as puberty changes a boy's larynx. The larynx enlarges, lowering the voice **permanently**. It is not known how large a dose will do this, but anything that is large enough to be therapeutic will deepen your voice, put a ceiling on your high range, and roughen the passaggios. Androgens are just the ticket if you are FtM trans. Otherwise, just don't go there. It can be disastrous for sopranos and high mezzos.

The effects of lower testosterone levels on men over forty is still up for debate, as the levels only drop one or two percent. At puberty, testosterone causes the vocal folds to thicken and lengthen. In older men there is a thinning of the vocal fold mass so perhaps Testosterone Replacement Therapy (TRT) could be beneficial, except that a 2009 study published in the *New England Journal of Medicine* was stopped early because the men on TRT had more than four times the number of cardiovascular problems.

It should also be noted that the gel from TRT easily transfers from the men using it to women, children, and even pets. The worst-case scenarios have included facial hair, sudden deepening of the voice, and stopped cycles in women, early puberty in children, and increased aggression in everyone.

Reflux

Gastroesophageal Reflux Disease (GERD)

Reflux, also known as heartburn, is a side-effect of some medications, and is generally more common later in life as we begin to lose muscle tone in the esophageal sphincter. In the rare instance that conversation lags in a group of voice professionals, toss the golden apple of reflux onto the table then enjoy the fireworks as the opinions fly back and forth.

We all experience reflux occasionally, but soloists dread that acidic wash brought on by nerves just before singing. It is like encasing a runner's legs in ice just before their race. There was a long list of what I would not eat on the day of a performance, and a short list of bland foods I depended on to keep reflux at bay. General symptoms of reflux/heartburn/GERD are the burning sensation in the chest, a chronic dry cough, feeling that there is a lump in your throat, hoarseness, asthma, laryngitis, earaches, bad breath, and a sudden increase in saliva.

Now there is Gaviscon® to ameliorate the less intense heartburn and reflux, there are homeopathics with alginate, and there are prescription medications and protocols for more severe reflux. These should be explored with your laryngologist. Do be careful about interactions between some reflux medications and Prozac or Celexa. Again, talk with your physician, and DO NOT make the mistake of self-diagnosing reflux and silent reflux, as there can be other things going on with similar symptoms.

Silent reflux or laryngopharyngeal reflux (LPR)

LPR is similar to GERD, but the symptoms are different. Babies have LPR because the esophageal sphincters are not yet developed. Adults get it when those same sphincters weaken and stomach acid travels up into the back of the throat, or even to the larynx and the back nasal airway. Silent reflux occurs mostly during sleep and causes inflammation when stomach acids travel where they don't belong.

The symptoms in adults tend to be more vague than with regular reflux/heartburn/GERD, including hoarseness, roughness when you first start to vocalize, trouble swallowing, persistent cough and excessive throat clearing, postnasal drip, extra throat mucus, a lump in the throat, sore throat, and recurrent ear infections. It is not easy to diagnose, and tests include scoping and pH monitoring which involves wearing a scope for 24 hours which may or may not catch your silent reflux activity.

As with regular reflux, there are dietary restrictions and the recommendations to stop eating three hours before sleep, lose weight and elevate the head of the bed four to six inches. Then things get serious with proton pump inhibitors, H2 blockers, and whatever you and your physician can find that works. On the homeopathic side, I have heard of a pill that blocks the sphincter overnight to keep the stomach gases from rising to the larynx.

Reflux laryngitis

Inflammation from when severe reflux sends stomach fluids all the way up to the vocal folds. This can be severe enough to cause scarring on the vocal folds.

Singing with an upper respiratory problem or a cold

This is when you are most likely to do damage, because the vocal folds are swollen. Ironically, the aging voice is not as vulnerable and for elderly men whose vocal folds have lost mass, the edema in the vocal folds can sometimes make singing easier. This is not to say one should look to sing while sick. It is never a good idea, and your fellow performers will not appreciate you sharing your germs with them.

Laryngitis

Your illness has progressed to laryngitis, and you are irreplaceable. The show must go on and all that. First, be absolutely sure that you are irreplaceable. Most of the time there is another solution if you look for it. You should not be singing on laryngitis, as it can be damaging to your vocal folds and will severely delay your recovery time. Would you run a race on a sprained ankle? If you make the decision to take steroids, be sure that you are given the steroids by mouth, NOT by inhaler. As stated above, a speaker or singer should never be given steroids with an inhaler, as they will sit on the vocal folds which are already in a compromised state.

Vitamin B12

Ever since it has been offered, there are elite singers who will have a shot of B12 before performances, believing it gives them greater energy and strength and adds ease and responsiveness to their voice. At the writing of this book, there are a survey study and clinical trials in progress at University of Southern California (USC) spearheaded by

Dr. Michael Johns looking at the effects of B12 on the voice. The results of the survey showed that thirty percent of Speech and Language Pathologists (SLPs), vocalists, and teachers all thought there was a benefit to the voice from taking vitamin B12, but none of the laryngologists agreed. And be aware that whereas B12 gives some people an energy boost, it makes other people lethargic.

There is a simple blood test to measure the amount of B vitamins in your body which would be wise to use, as self-medicating is not completely harmless. The author spoke with a professional singer and teacher in her fifties who had been taking high dosages of B6 as part of her treatment for Lyme's Disease and developed B6 toxicity which included peripheral neuropathy, brain fog, liver damage, and a raspy, out-of-control voice. She is slowly working her way back to her voice, balance in her B vitamin levels, and a healthy body.

Common sense warning

It is always a good idea to tread carefully. It is easy to assume that if a small amount of something is good, then a large amount is better. That is not a safe assumption. We can also have blind trust in 'natural' and homeopathic remedies, without checking what they are actually composed of and what they do in the body. There can be hidden androgens in the mix, or there can be ingredients that duplicate prescription medications and thus substantially increase your dosage. It is your body – do your homework, ask questions, research online and pay attention to how your body is reacting to what you put into it, be it medicine, supplements, foods, or liquids.

Information sources

Information for this chapter was gleaned from papers, lectures, and panels presented at The Voice Foundation Symposia, and from the informative, interactive (and free!), online National Association of Teachers of Singing series of 'NATS Chats' interviews with Dr. Robert T. Sataloff, and with Margaret Baroody and Dr. Michael Johns. Dr. Johns has also kindly been available to read through and consult on this chapter.

5

Back to the studio

Karen Brunssen

This chapter will focus on circumstances that bring serious singers, professional, semi-professional, and amateur, back to the private vocal studio, what and how to evaluate their vocal situation, and help them deal with the multiple perspectives and realities of singing as a senior citizen.

My overall area of interest is "the evolving singing voice which is profound at every age." As a living musical instrument from birth through old age, vocal function is dependent on where the body is within chronological development and change. Many of these changes take place slowly, while others can happen more quickly. Throughout our lives we should learn to sing within our limits, not below and not beyond them. Studying the "what and why" of age-related vocal limits and expectations, as they relate to changes within our bodies throughout our lifetime, is fascinating and enlightening. It offers explanations for why we can do some things at one time, and why we can't at another. Generally speaking, the longest period of hormonal stability for women is after puberty for approximately four decades. For men the hormonal changes happen very slowly from the ages of forty to sixty and then faster. We are never stagnant in the aging process during these decades, but generally one can experience dependable vocal production from the early twenties (or so) into the fifties, which some refer to as "prime-time". Currently, vocal pedagogy classes taken during college years deal with how to sing during the "prime-time". Students study pictures of the adult larynx, discuss the adult proportions of the resonator, vibrator and respiration, and have expectations for the acoustics of optimal professional singers as their vocal goal. There are many differences between the adult singer and infant, child, pubescent, and older singers that merit consideration and comparison. As baby boomers in the United States become senior citizens at the rate of 65,000 per day and are living longer, there is a demand to remain vocally active. There is a call and a need for information about singing into one's senior years.

First efforts to train the adult voice often start at the beginning of the forty years of hormonal stability. It is typical that aspiring young singers work very hard to train their voices by taking voice lessons that started perhaps in high school and/or during their college years. For some, that is the end of their vocal study, although they continue to value their singing voices. Many use their voices as music teachers, in choruses, and for occasional solo opportunities while a few seek to study vocal performance privately or through graduate schools. This further study involves working with excellent teachers, coaching with collaborative pianists who specialize in vocal repertoire, auditioning and taking part in summer programs, apprentice programs, and an array of learning and performing opportunities. Their youthful energy coincides with ongoing physical development that finally reaches a point of stability in the late twenties. Through this period their attainable musical possibilities incrementally grow due to a combination of vocal insight, neuromuscular development, and the natural stabilization of the vocal instrument. The smart young singer, with guidance from teachers and coaches, can aggressively pursue their art form while also maintaining vocal comfort and health, along with realistic and "age-optimal" expectations. The anxious, impatient, aggressive young singer will be frustrated, blaming themselves or others for not being able to attain professional musical demands, missing the fact that their human growth is a factor as well.

The third and fourth decades of life are generally stable periods of life for both men and women. Once the voice settles in and a vocal career is established, be it full-time or part-time, professional or amateur, as a chorister for church or synagogue choirs, local community performance opportunities, or as a professional soloist in oratorio, concert, recital, light-opera, or opera, many singers tend to study voice less often and as they have time, money, and/or needs based on upcoming repertoire. Wise singers make an effort to keep their voices on a professional track with ongoing vocal study. The rigors of regularly singing alongside fellow excellent singers, under the baton of great conductors, doing demanding repertoire, and getting ready for auditions offers a comparative, dynamic professional environment that continually invigorates, evaluates, tests, exercises, and challenges the virtuosic musical and vocal demands for singers. Excellence in all five textures of singing; legato, staccato, coloratura, messa di voce, and articulation, is attainable at a high level during this time, but rarely on one's own. The serious singer needs constant input from voice professionals.

For women, menopause can be the cause of significant changes in the voice suddenly or gradually. (See Dr. Barbara Fox DeMaio's chapter, "The Menopausal Voice – Singing Through the Storm") For men, the level of testosterone, which affects muscle strength, lowers very gradually up until the age of sixty and then more quickly in the next decade.

It varies significantly according to each person as to when it becomes noticeably more difficult to attain the professional standards they were able to achieve during the "prime years" of singing. Sometimes the singer realizes it themselves. Other times, another set of ears brings it to their attention. Both are almost always a humbling realization for the singer and can be frustrating and confusing. A few singers study voice regularly or semi-regularly, but many more do not, and changes having to do with age may have nothing to do with whether one takes lessons or not. Some have not felt a vocal need and may have schedules and budgets that preclude making the effort to take lessons. Noticing the changes can range anywhere from a slight notion that they don't feel as in-shape as before, to having difficulty singing certain repertoire. It can be a "crisis" due to less than positive results at an audition, or it can be hearing their own facility change in comparison to those they are singing with. Whatever the reason, something is different than it used to be. A change in reality prompts students in their fifth and sixth decade of life to return to the voice studio. At this point a teacher who understands what can and cannot be done to help the aging voice is a great help for a struggling singer. Facts about normal aging can serve as a helpful, impartial means of explanation during what is always a very personal time for the singer.

Step 1: Getting to know them

The first step in a voice lesson at this juncture is to listen to what the student has to say and what they are concerned about or hoping for. Serious singers have egos and pride in their accomplishments. For decades they have acquired a great amount of experience, skills, language, and repertoire. They have devoted their hearts, minds, and bodies to singing. Their singing experiences are alive within them. They have persevered with busy schedules beyond the typical 9–5 work schedule. They love singing and want to keep doing it as long as possible; they want anything or anyone that is stopping that from happening to be dealt with, and quickly. They are likely quite emotional about this at some level and may be in denial about their own vocal condition. They may bring with them medical issues they have gone through: reflux, heart problems, balance issues, physical injuries that hinder their ability to stand, depression, vision, back problems, cancer, medication, surgery, etc. It is very rare that someone has not gone through some sort of medical issue by this point in their life. As they talk, ask questions that will help them offer more information. Some will handle all of this bravely. Some tend to be unaware of what the problem is. Some may become a little sad. Some might even break down. They are talking about themselves, and nothing is more personal. What I have experienced during this part of their first lesson when dealing with their older singing, is that they are also very relieved to have someone to talk to about it candidly. It is often a comfort to them when they understand that normal physical changes are taking place. Facing reality is the name of the game. For the teacher: CONFIDENTIALITY IS A MUST!

> How long since you last took a voice lesson?
> What are the ongoing issues with your voice according to teachers you have studied with?
> What brings you here today?
> What medications do you take and do you notice any effects on your voice from them?
> Any surgeries?
> Do you take hormone replacement therapy?
> What changes have been pointed out to you?
> What changes do you notice?
> Are there any ongoing medical issues?
> Where do you currently sing?
> How many hours a week do you sing?
> Do you practice?
> What are your goals in coming here today?
> What is your daily work?
> How much water do you drink in a day?
> Do you smoke? How much?
> Do you drink? How much?

Step 2: Evaluation

The next step is to hear them sing and discern the reality of their vocalism as compared to their own perspective about their voice. Often it takes very little time to hear the problems. Sometimes it takes until the extremes of the range, both lower and higher, before noticing issues. I prefer to diagnose using simple mono-syllabled exercises at the very start.

> 5-4-3-2-1 on "ee" for women and "aye" for men.

One can easily diagnose with a song as well, but I like to have concepts established in the exercises and then carry those into a song.

Typical problems one will hear from older serious voice students may include:

- Loss of range (up and/or down)
- Slow vibrato
- Need for frequent breaths
- Breathy sound
- Colorless sound
- A large break
- "Knerdly" sound and other compensatory effort
- High larynx sounds
- Intonation
- Awkward flexibility on coloratura
- Awkward flexibility going from loud to soft
- Cramping at the top of their range

The reasons behind each of these varies from person to person. Sometimes the reason is due to a technical issue and sometimes it requires a doctor's care, and not necessarily a laryngologist.

Step 3: Remediation

Although remediation is the next topic, in my lessons those start to happen within the initial few repetitions of the first exercise. I can establish potential for improvements right away by fixing the tongue position of their "ee" or "aye" vowel. I can show them they have little h's between notes and that is "illegal". It takes very little explanation to improve these things, and they often notice a positive or new change that they may need to become familiar and comfortable with. A better vowel plus a better legato equals improvement! Then begin work to remediate what can be remediated, showing them ways to improve.

Be honest about where they are, what they have and don't have control over, and how to stay in the best possible shape going forward.

Step 4: Application

As I meet with serious singers whose vocal challenges may be totally age-related or a combination of technical and aging issues, I encourage them to be realistic. They have options as far as their future singing goes. They can address deficiencies and renew some degree of their professional-quality voice so they can continue with their current status of singing if marked improvements become evident. Or they can self-select to leave a professional situation and move on to a doable singing situation where they are valued and appreciated for their older optimal singing voice as it is now.

Sometimes the task of starting to work on the voice after dealing with the realities of aging seems to be an impossible task. At the end of the lesson I will often ask, "What are you going to take home with you today?" It puts the onus on them to comprehend, interpret and apply what we have worked on. The amount of time needed to train singing is very similar to the amount of time recommended for overall exercise: Minimum of four times a week for twenty minutes to maintain, and more to improve. To help make their initial efforts accessible, attainable, and with guaranteed improvement, I give these students ONE "5 Day Mini-Challenge."

5 day mini-challenges (choose one)

- 5 days of talking with a headier sound
- 5 days of walking taller
- 5 days of semi-occluded exercises
- 5 days with the straw
- 5 days of pondering the inner smile
- 5 days of feeling the muscles of breathing when sitting while you sing
- 5 days of including staccato exercises
- 5 days of all 5 vocal textures

Don't promise them the moon. Every person is different. Some maintain a lot of their prior vocal achievements, and some don't. There are singers on YouTube performing in their eighties, nineties, and older who sound amazing. There is a 103-year-old soprano who does sound older, but we think it's cool that she is still singing. Even Florence Foster Jenkins was 72 when she recorded her album.

In addition to the singing voice itself, there are the realities of peripheral issues that make it harder to continue to sing and perform such as medical issues, plus changes in hearing, vision, balance, and the ability to stand for a long time.

Learn about your voice. It is interesting to be able to make mindful choices like:

Mindful choices

- Feed the head voice, starve the chest voice
- No Kermit (swallowing relaxes those muscles)
- Research shows that even a little work on muscles helps

- Singing beyond limitations is counterproductive no matter what age
- Encourage needed muscles
- Discourage compensatory muscles
- Relax the larynx when taking a breath
- Use creaking (imitating the sound of a creaking door with a squeaky "ee" sound)
- Inner smile – pharyngeal stretch
- Various exercises for the five textures of singing; legato, staccato, coloratura, messa di voce, and articulation
- Practice onset exercises
- Snore when breathing to relax throat
- Use a "wolf tone" (sort of a breathy "huh" that you feel in your chest, below the larynx) to relax laryngeal position

Mindful concepts for practicing and performing

- Tongue dead and spread
- Relax larynx with each breath
- Palate up and pharynx wide
- Neck dilated rather than stretched up and long
- Think about where the voice is going
- Ponder about where the voice comes from
- Be smart about amount, manner, spacing of singing
- Divorce tongue from sound
- Clever, slight vowel modification
- Jokes + laughter = high palates
- Cheekbones up
- Arch and width of pharynx on higher notes
- Sing in the position of inhalation
- Sing as if surprised
- Sing with a smile in the back of the throat
- Sing in the position of the start of a yawn
- Use it or lose it!

The following are four mindful bundles for various challenges found with aging voices (but not exclusive to aging voices). They state the problem, what the physical issue could be that is causing the problem, exercises that will help, and the mindful concept involved. They can be done as five-day mini-challenges:

Bundle #1

- Flatting, loss of vocal color
- Palate less responsive
- Hands on chest and do pharyngeal stretches
- Palate up and pharynx wide, feed the head voice, starve the chest voice, cheek bones up, smile, yawn, inhalation, surprised, like opening your ears on the airplane
- Do pharyngeal stretches twice a day for 5 days

Bundle #2

- Lack of clarity
- Muscles of breathing weaken
- MMM, ZZZ or VVV noticing support muscles while sitting, SSS to ZZZ, and creaking
- Encourage needed muscles
- While doing typical daily activity, do and think about MMM, ZZZ or VVV in various rhythms

Bundle #3

- Breathy Attack
- Vocal cords may be slack, and support muscles not
- Do onset exercises. Creaking may help.
- This is a very fine motor skill that needs careful coordination, concentration, and repetition. You may notice your support muscles begin to cooperate more dependably.
- While doing typical daily activity stop four times a day for 5 minutes and do onset exercises.

Bundle #4

- Vocal Stamina
- Muscles of breathing weaken
- "mmm", "zzz" or "vvv" noticing support muscles while sitting, "sss" to "zzz", and creaking
- Encourage needed muscles
- Any effort to exercises will be helpful

Examples from the studio

A sixty-two-year-old bass baritone seemed to have difficulty supporting his voice. He explained that he had a little light-headedness due to a heart condition that was being monitored. We did exercises to increase awareness of how it feels to relax certain muscles for the inhalation and engage them for exhalation first on the unvoiced "ssss", then on a voiced "zzzz". By putting his fists on the sides of his body he could focus on how the oblique muscles work. By sitting on a chair and leaning forward he could feel the engagement and release of the low oblique muscles down to the pubic bone. Leaning against the back of the chair he could feel how even muscles in the back are involved in support. This exercised those muscles collectively while drawing attention to them individually. Then he sang a 54321 scale on "zzzz" further coordinating and developing each muscle group. Finally, we changed it to "zay" and challenged it further by adding pulses on each note 555 444 333 222 1111111. We followed with "zay 123454321" so he could experience the more fluid results and better facility using a "mindful" exercise process. This was applied to other exercises and repertoire. Improvement was significant from both my perspective and his. After about eight months, his doctor decided it was time to do a procedure for his heart. When he returned from a few months of recovery, I was amazed at the beauty of his rolling sound as more oxygen was literally flowing through him now. This is a good example of the combination of focusing on an area of vocal technique and what 21st century medical procedures can correct.

In another instance a very regular professional student in his early fifties came back, after a couple of months being away, with incredible vocal improvement. Whatever he had done was making his singing easier, more stable, and thrilling. Was there a new teacher out there with an idea I wanted to learn about? The answer turned out to be that he was evaluated and diagnosed for sleep apnea. He had been sleeping with a c-pap machine for six weeks and the vocal change was exciting. This prompted me to be evaluated also, and I experienced a similar limbering up of the voice as well as fewer sinus issues. A year later I was re-evaluated and my sleep number was lowered from 16 to 11. The doctor explained that the pharyngeal tissue literally changes when it is not disturbed so much through the snoring, so I did not have as much interference and a lower setting was appropriate. Two other people, one in his fifties and one in his sixties, were prompted by our success stories to be evaluated as well. They experienced the increase in overall energy that is typical after getting real sleep thanks to the c-pap machine, along with better vocal function. Plenty of oxygen is a good thing for singing, and for life in general.

A sixty-year-old female who had majored in voice in college, is now a voice teacher, and has sung professionally in choruses part-time for over thirty years, was informed that she would need to do a follow-up re-audition with the hopes that she might have a chance to remediate a now extremely breathy tone. Throughout her life she had a slight tendency for bowed vocal cords. Through the years she took voice lessons as needed before bi-annual auditions. We learned that instead of causing air pressure that will encourage the vocal cords to vibrate, she was working with all her might to blow more air through the vocal cords. Her efforts were well intentioned and based on "letting the breath move through". However, that was almost the opposite of what she needed to do. We worked on isolated exercising and understanding of the muscles of breathing (as described with the bass-baritone above). That helped to some degree. Then we added some "creaking". It was not easy for her to do because of the bowing. After experimenting for a while, she figured out how to make that noise, and eventually could creak up and down on lower notes. We started to sing 54321 on "zee" and gradually the voice started to clear. She is now a faithful creaker, which is helpful to her as someone who tends toward bowed vocal cords. As we age the vocal cords can become slack and do not offer as much resistance to air. Creaking can help this. I creak regularly myself and am always better for it.

In another situation a soprano in her early fifties was encouraged to take some lessons as her voice had lost color. Both the mindful work on the support muscles and the creaking were helpful. However, in addition, she was over-opening her mouth. Therefore, the tone lacked desirable professional ringing harmonics and muscles of the neck were overly involved. It was completely counter-intuitive for her to close her mouth, but whenever she did the neck relaxed and the overtones were evident in the room. They were not evident to her though, and she missed her spirited efforts to sing with a very open mouth that moved for every note as she sang. It can be very difficult, considering decades of successful professional experience, to have to relearn a throat position.

A woman in her early fifties came to me claiming to be a high, light soprano, but for some reason, over a short period of time, couldn't go up into her higher register anymore. She would get to an F5 at the top of the staff and not much further. I could not figure out, despite trying much of my bag of tricks, why she had such problems. The voice just seemed to quit. I did not hear evidence of swelling but had no idea what was going on. After three voice lessons I suggested she have her vocal folds looked at. She went to a very good laryngologist and was diagnosed with "estrogen depletion" both by what the laryngologist saw and then by her ob-gyn doctor. She started taking hormone replacement therapy and the issue was significantly remediated three weeks later when she came back for a lesson. She vocalized easily to a high D6, which was not as high as she went as a young singer, but a sixth above what I had heard three weeks earlier.

6

Structural maintenance and aerobic breath

Martha Howe

The voice is breath; moving, vibrating air, bouncing off the surfaces of the throat, tongue, palates, and teeth, and employing resonating spaces in your vocal tract, head, and face on its way out the door. When there is muscle tension, it creates obstacles in this path. These obstacles can result in a feeling of clumsiness, of the voice suddenly stumbling over itself. Variable or insufficient air flow can result in a weak or wobbly sound. Tension can also cause pitch and range problems, leaving the speaker or singer vocally tired.

Phonating (producing vocal sound) is beautifully complex, and the following is a very basic overview: To produce pitch, phonation, air comes up from the lungs to under the vocal folds (the sub-glottis) and the appropriate amount is propelled across the vocal folds to create the vibration for a particular pitch. This process includes movement in the larger cartilages of the larynx, and the interaction between tiny sensors below and around the vocal folds with the tiny arytenoids which stretch and release the vocal folds. This vibrating air (sounding rather like a duck call or the buzzing through a brass mouthpiece) begins the journey through the vocal tract (the space from the vocal folds or glottis, through the throat, all along the tongue and mouth to your lips). Vowels are formed as the sound is pushed into different shapes by the tongue and palates, and your particular sound qualities are the end result of the shape and length of your vocal tract. I like to say that consonants are the final accessories a word puts on as it heads out the door.

This all runs, like a magic act, faster than our brains could command the individual bits to interact and respond to each other, so it is run by the involuntary control system (those parts of our body that tick along, doing their tasks, keeping us alive).

Where we do definitely affect the process, is by pushing too much air through, or not having enough air available to, that which creates pitch. Also, when there is excess tension in the throat, jaw, lips, and tongue it will mess with the vocal tract's ability to do its job effectively and efficiently. Speaking and singing are full-body activities. Pain, especially in your neck, shoulders or back, can affect your ability to breathe and it also translates into increased tension in your jaw. Suddenly you are getting hoarse and you don't know why. This chapter looks at both the physical side of addressing tension, posture and breath, plus the intentional side of noticing thoughts and habits that are counterproductive.

Physical tension, posture, and the voice

If you stub your toe, you will change the way you walk until the pain goes away. If your shoulder hurts, it will change how you lift your arm. Throughout life, we alter our posture and movement to compensate for discomfort, stiffness, or limitations in our bodies. We have various pains in our joints or muscles, plus referred pain from subluxations of the spine, and all the tension that we carry in our shoulders, neck, and jaw which ultimately effects our singing. Spinal subluxations will be reflected in our posture, flexibility, and our ability to breathe freely and deeply. As we age, these changes become less subtle, and what was a minor compensation can become set in stone. Arthritis, injuries, and calcifications can alter our skeletal structure. It is important to address these issues sooner rather than later, when the resulting jaw, neck and facial tensions can make us vulnerable to hoarseness, limited range, shortness of breath, weakness of speaking or singing tone, or the dreaded wobble.

There are many different ways to work on structural balance, posture, and breath, and we are often led to the perfect consultant or therapist just when we need them. Look around you and see what is available. The following is an alphabetical list of introductory overviews of a few of the different modalities that people find useful to alleviate tension and pain:

Alexander Technique

Wikipedia states that it is 'an educational process that attempts to develop the ability to avoid unnecessary muscular tension by retraining physical movement. Alexander believed that poor habits in posture and movement damaged spatial self-awareness; he believed the technique was a mental training technique as well'. If you have experienced the benefits of Alexander Technique work, you understand the impact these sessions have on your body, breath, posture, alignment, and the physical integration of the voice. I was lucky enough to be led to it in the 1980s, and found it to be wonderfully freeing, releasing my posture and movements while opening my breath. I continue to use some of the principles in my studio, and regularly recommend Alexander Technique work to performers or anyone who wants to better understand their body.

Chiropractic

There are many different methods gathered under the general banner of 'chiropractic'. Some Doctors of Chiropractic (DCs) manipulate the joints (manually or with an adjuster) of the neck, torso, back, hips, ankles, feet, face, arms, and hands. Other DCs work on the subtle levels and meridians, using light touch on energy matrixes and pressure points to release blockages in the body's flow of energy so that a body can correct and heal itself. Network and Bio-Geometric Integration (BGI) are two of the better-known techniques that do not use manual force in adjustments.

The field of chiropractic continues to expand, including kinesiology and sports focus, and sometimes you can find a DC who has worked with voice professionals and understands their particular needs. I was lucky enough to find a DC with an office just behind Carnegie Hall in New York City who regularly adjusted the front ribs which could be thrown out of alignment with sneezing or energetic breathing. She also adjusted feet which helped tremendously with overall energy flow. Most chiropractors will employ a combination of methods that they are comfortable with, tailoring adjustments to what each patient needs and wants. It is important to find a DC whose background and methodology you are comfortable with.

Feldenkrais Method

Feldenkrais has two lesson structures; Awareness Through Movement (ATM) which is a group lesson with guided movements, and Functional Integration (FI) which is a hands-on session with a practitioner. The Feldenkrais Method seeks to reprogram those movements that, because of faulty initial learning, injuries, or structural problems, are clumsy or inefficient. Moshe Feldenkrais, D.Sc, developed this method of re-wiring the nervous system to prevent being confined to a wheelchair by his knee injuries. A black-belt in judo, he used his knowledge of judo, anatomy, physics, physiology, and kinesiology to study the function of movement.

The use of imagination, the attention to control, tension and release, and resulting development of neuroplasticity, all make this a very effective method for developing an awareness of what is actually going on in your body. This is extremely useful for all voice users and professionals, especially as we age and need to listen ever more closely to our bodies.

The Feldenkrais Method is better known in Europe than in the U.S., but one introductory book with extensive exercises and clear instructions is, *Singing with Your Whole Self, A Singer's Guide to Feldenkrais Awareness through Movement*, Second Edition, by Samuel H. Nelson and Elizabeth L. Blades, published by Rowman & Littlefield.

Myofascial release therapy

Myofascial tissue is the tough membrane that wraps, supports, and connects the muscles. The therapist will be locating stiff 'trigger points' in the myofascial tissue then using gentle, sustained, manual pressure and stretching to release the restriction and restore elasticity to the myofasciae. This frees up muscle and joint movement, while indirectly reducing pain.

Stress seems to be a constant in life and we generally store most of the tension from that stress in our jaws, necks, and shoulders. Myofascial release therapy can help release this tension and loosen the muscles. If you learn it from an expert practitioner, you can also self-massage your face, jaw, and neck fasciae and muscles to release tension.

Neuro-fascial release

A light-touch Osteopathic manipulation developed by Stephen Myles Davidson, D.O. in 1987. It focuses on the nerve-fasciae interface, locating the irritated tracts of nerve tissues, helping the receptors and neuromuscular bundles heal, then altering the brain-maps/memories, using light pressure on a release point so that the patient's own body does the releasing. The therapist's intention, skill, touch, intuition, and knowledge of anatomy are very important. This light-touch can also release emotional patterns tied to traumatic experiences that have imprinted in the connective tissue, thus allowing the body to heal itself.

Tension from thoughts and emotions

Structural problems and injuries are not the only ways that energy becomes blocked, stopped, or held in our bodies. More subtle, but quite powerful culprits are our thoughts, beliefs, memories, and fears. Take a moment and remember something that makes you angry. Did your jaw tighten? Your teeth clench? What happens in your throat when you are sad? It is now understood that energy from traumatic and emotionally charged moments in life will get caught in our bodies. Being alive means gathering greater and greater amounts of these charged moments and storing them in our emotional bodies.

Our thoughts alone are a source of obstruction and tension. Think about someone who truly irritates you. Why do they do those things? Why do they insist on that? How can they think like that? Notice your jaw, tongue, and throat muscles. What about the muscles around your mouth and eyes? What is your breath doing?

Now, take a moment to think about a beloved pet, or someone amusing you are fond of. Think about how much you love it when they do something silly, how sweet it is to just watch them.

Notice what shifted in your jaw, tongue, throat and face. Is it easier or harder to breathe? This could be very interesting, depending on your reactions.

I discovered the power of thoughts, that inner soundtrack, when creating characters for stage. Whatever train of thought I repeated inside my head affected my face, posture, movements, and tonal color. It changed how I inhabited my body. All of those things we say to ourselves, the judgments, the opinions, the snarkiness to yourself and others, it all creates flecks of tension. These flecks add up over time and have a direct impact on your voice, as that energy and tension is stored in your shoulders, neck, jaw, throat, tongue and face. If you do not actively release this tension, it settles in and solidifies.

Tension release

One of effective way to release tension is through our breath, with an exhalation. Simply inhaling to a count of four, and exhaling to a count of eight will help, and has been shown to lower blood pressure. It is a starting point. This simple breathing practice also tones the vagus nerve which is a primary nerve system for breathing and creating sound.

Meditation

If you do not already have a meditation practice, look for a breath-based, peaceful meditation. For beginners, 'led' meditations, where an adept meditator describes a journey or scene during the meditation, can be especially helpful to focus your busy thoughts. Expect your thoughts to jump around, there is a reason our thoughts are affectionately called the Monkey Mind. You are looking for meditations that will allow you to observe your thoughts, observe your breath, and that will help release thoughts, breath, and tension. Shop around and trust your instincts and intuition.

Singing for fun

Whether in a group, a choir, in structured lessons, or privately to yourself during the day, the physical act of singing releases both pleasure hormones and healing hormones. If you can keep your inner-judge/critic at bay, giving yourself permission to just relax, breathe, and sing, then there can be an effective release of tension. Studies have shown that having fun making music can reverse a good percentage of the changes in our DNA caused by prolonged stress. Singing releases dopamine, serotonin, and endo-cannabinoids so you can feel better emotionally and physically.

General breathing practices

Have you ever been cleaning out a closet and as soon as you see something from your past, you experience a flood of memories and emotions? Your body is like that closet, and there are knots of memories and emotions that get released when triggered. Some of them are lovely, some of them more challenging. These knots can sit there, pouring out emotions, memories, and judgements when triggered, or they can be released and neutralized through energy work, breath, meditation, and mindfulness.

Often, we will stuff emotion that can't be dealt with in the moment under our breath. Later, when you begin to breathe deeply, the emotions will release. It is much better to get the knots out of there, but it is also a primary reason many people avoid taking a good, cleansing, rejuvenating breath. They are subconsciously wary of the Pandora's Box that may open. When emotions surface from under the breath, it is not necessary to know WHY you are sad or upset, that is just old story around the emotion. You can simply keep breathing and let the emotions wash out in the exhalation. It can be helpful to visualize the inhalation as a power-wash, cleaning out your lungs and torso. Send the exhalation into beautiful, sparkly light and it will clear faster.

Through millennia, paying attention to your breath has been a pathway to peacefulness, mindfulness, and quieting your inner critic, while offering relief from stress, negative thoughts, and depression. Yogic breath exercises are very good for releasing stress and clearing out those knots of old energy.

Pranayama and pranic breathing

There are excellent breathing practices taught in yoga studios and with pranic-focused meditation practices. To go into them in depth would require another book, as the breathing techniques are as varied as the yogis and yoginis teaching them. If your yoga teacher does not incorporate your breathing into the stretches (asanas), then they have missed the point.

Prana is the sanskrit word for a life-force/energy flowing within everything, similar to the concept of Chi. The various pranayamas (yogic breathing practices) balance energy flow in the body, feed prana, release tension, and vitalize energy. They also counter stress and stress hormones, calming and focusing the mind and strengthening the lungs. The information found online is varied and variable, and like meditation, it is best and safest to learn techniques from someone who is adept and respects the power and properties of the various pranayamas.

When you breathe in through your nose, and out through your mouth, it is easier to release tension, and this method will calm things down, especially when the exhalation is much longer than the inhalation.

Yogic alternate nostril breathing

This helps you to feel the air from your inhalation moving the ribs and the back, and is good for centering. It also balances two main vertical energy meridians in your torso. (The Ida and Pingala that wind around the Shushumna nadi.):

- Place your right hand in front of your face, index and middle fingers between eyebrows

- Press your thumb on the right side of your nose. and ring finger on the left side of your nosePress against the left side of your nose with the ring finger to close it offBreathe in the right nostril for a beat of around 6, hold the breath inside for 3

- Release the ring finger and block the right side of your nose instead, pressing against the side of your nose with your thumb

- Breathe out your left nostril to a count of 6 or more

- Hold for a count of 3, then breathe in the left nostril for a count of 6 or more

- Hold the breath inside for a count of 3

- Switch fingers (block left, release right), breathe out right, breathe in right, hold, switch, etc.

The counting is to help center and slow you down, until you fall into your natural rhythm. The thumb and ring finger only switch after the inhalation, when you are full of air.

Ocean breath

It helps develop your awareness of the flow of breath, and is good for noticing how and when the inhalation and exhalation turn naturally:

- As you relax the hinge where your jaw hooks on to your skull, you should feel a release in tongue tension. When relaxed, the tongue sits high in the mouth, near the hard palate or roof of the mouth

- As you inhale and exhale, your breath flows between the roof of your mouth and your relaxed tongue, and will make a sound like the ocean

- During your inhalation, imagine a wave building and cresting. When you are full of air, float for a moment or two, enjoying the anticipation at the top of the cresting wave

- With the exhalation, picture the wave curling and rolling into shore, where it dissipates in the sand. Let the cycle pause for a moment and wait for the natural turn to the next inhalation

- Just as ocean waves have a rhythm and are not rushed, let your body lead and show you a comfortable, relaxed speed for the cycle. Observe and enjoy the rhythm of the breath

- The Ocean breath can be very peaceful but breathing in and out through the mouth intensifies emotions, like adding fuel to a fire, in conversations or heated discussions. You will also notice that in those situations your inhalations may rise up towards your shoulders instead of staying down in the lungs where they belong.

When you breathe in and out through the nose, the energy becomes quite powerful. This is called the 'Fire' or 'Bellows' breath, and the faster it is the more intense it becomes. <u>People with high blood pressure should never practice these methods, as they have been shown to elevate blood pressure.</u>

Prolonged, rapid-breath therapy

Breath is a very powerful way to release tension, and to direct energy. Prolonged, rapid, deep breathing is an excellent way to release old, caught emotions and heal from trauma. It is also essential that the person guiding this process knows what they are doing and respects the power of this kind of breath therapy. It is not a party trick, and people with high blood pressure could be in danger.

It is also good to do a more exploratory method to raise body awareness. I first encountered the following process through Network Chiropractic which led me to Epstein and Altman's book, *The 12 Stages of Healing*. Breath balancing helps identify when you are breathing in the high chest, middle ribs, or belly, how they each feel, and how to balance them. As with all breath work, you may be surprised by emotions coming from 'nowhere'. Remember to let them flow out with the exhalation. Although emotions can feel huge and overwhelming, like clouds they are always moving and passing through. They only camp out and settle in when we resist them. That wonderful feeling of clarity and release 'after the storm' is so sweet when we let them go.

Breath balancing

- Lie on your back, with your knees bent, feet on the floor (like an old-fashioned sit-up)
- Place both hands over your belly button, palms down, one palm directly on top of the other palm
- Inhale so your belly fills and moves your palms up, then exhale so your belly and palms release back down. (As much as possible, just move the belly when breathing)
- Do this several times and feel if it is easy for you, or if it feels blocked
- Then move your hands to your upper chest (bronchial region), keeping palm over palm
- Inhale so the upper chest fills and moves up and down with the breath. (As much as possible, just move the upper chest)
- Keep breathing into the upper chest/bronchial area and notice what it feels like. Is it tight? Is it easy? Are there emotions that come up for you?
- Now move your hands to the mid-point on your torso (evenly between the first two locations) where the breath will move the ribs and intercostal muscles. Keep palm over palm, both palms down, facing your body
- Again, have your breath move your body, which moves your hands. (As much as possible, have your breathing just move the ribs and intercostal muscles)
- What do you feel? Which of these three areas is the easiest and most comfortable? Which is the hardest to move, or feels the most stuck or tight?
- Now, place one palm on the calmest/easiest area, and one palm on the tightest/most stuck. (Use whichever hand feels best on each location)

- Breathe into the 'easiest', and on the out-breath, feel that energy go through the body to the 'harder' location. Breathe in there, then on the out-breath send it back to the 'easy' hand. Following your own rhythm, send the energy and breath back and forth, palm to palm

- Listen to your breath, listen to your body as the breath flows palm to palm. Switch around between the three locations, let the inhalations and exhalations flow between them. The breath will start to balance itself, if you don't think about it too much and follow what you feel

Aerobic breath, focus and experience

Focusing on breath is a good place to start but will only get you so far. Whatever we focus on, must be distanced so that we can focus on it. You can focus on a pillow on the couch, or on the tree across the street, or on something you wish to study. If you focus on your breath, you will continue to observe it rather than experience it. Would you like to focus on the fudge or enjoy a piece? You can focus on the pillow, or you can sit down on the couch, relax into it, and enjoy the pillow.

Singing and strong speech require active breathing like you would use for dancing, rapid walking, tennis, and so forth. When you are standing or sitting, your body gives you normal, 'at rest' breathing, and we must convince the body that we actually need a more aerobic breath.

If you place a strong focus on the ribs, or the muscles of your breath, those areas will activate, but only as long as you are directly focused on them. This gets very frustrating, as there are so many things to distract us and pull our focus elsewhere. The moment you focus on the conductor, or your music, or what *are* those tenors doing? then the body immediately returns to its normal seated/standing non-energized breath.

What to do? Rather than observe your inhalation and exhalation from the safe distance of your head, try to experience how the inhalation and exhalation **feel** in your body. Easily said; not so easily done. So far, the best pathway into this experience that I've found, is to pay close attention to the physical sensations of the breath, following the experience of the inhalation and becoming fascinated by what is going on in your lungs, ribs, belly, and diaphragm. **Feel** your inhalation move the ribs, expanding them sideways (all the way around into your back). What is going on in your belly muscles? What are your shoulders up to? Be sure that the breath alone is moving things around. Unfortunately, we can get 'helpful' by expanding things ahead of the breath – if a little expansion is good, isn't a lot of expansion better? No. Your body knows exactly how much space is needed for whatever the task will be. Trust it and listen to it. Let the breath itself move the ribs and belly.

As we get older, we tend to not use our pulmonary system to its fullest. Not all of us get to the gym regularly, dance, jog, or walk rapidly enough to get our lungs pumping. Sometimes that big sigh is their only chance to stretch and 'clean house'. Singing is an excellent way to work the lungs, if you realize it is an aerobic activity and make sure that air is actually moving as you sing!

7

The aging voice: one singer's perspective

Martha L. Randall

When I was a young singer, I thought I would sing until I was fifty; when I became aware of the Voice Foundation, I thought I would sing until I was fifty and then participate in laboratory studies, with electrodes inserted into my vocal folds. Life has not turned out that way – I still sing for my students at 75, though my last public performance was in a faculty recital at age 68, and I have not connected with a voice lab to do the studies that still intrigue me. Each singer is different, and each aging singer is not only unique, but ages in a different way. When you have looked at one aging singer … you have looked at *one* aging singer!

There is a distinction between the aging voice and the aging singer. We can assume that if you are a singer, you have learned how to sing, so aging affects your ability to do what you have always been able to do. If you have always wanted to sing, but are taking it up later in life, you will be learning the basics of singing while accommodating the limitations of an older voice. Do not be discouraged! It is certainly possible to learn to sing and enjoy it. I am writing from one professional singer's perspective.

Many of the changes related to aging will be addressed elsewhere in this book and those tissue and hormonal changes cannot be denied, but I am going to focus on the mechanics. As we first notice the effects of aging in general, we joke about it – that all body parts are closer to the ground than they used to be, that we walk into a room and forget what we went to get, that we get distracted and absent-mindedly miss a turn. As the years pass, these events are not as funny as they used to be, but they are real. The good part of aging is that it happens gradually, and we adapt without even realizing it much of the time. The bad part about aging is that it is insidious, and the little habits that the young body forgives lay down a pattern of use that is limiting in the end. (I tell my students to behave in ways that their future bodies will thank them for, especially when I see them curled over their cell phones or sitting in the hall with laptops on their knees, backs rounded against the wall.) The face, when relaxed, droops much more, the ribs feel very comfortable in the unwound, downward position, and we find ourselves sitting in collapsed postures. These habits can be recognized and changed, if not fully corrected – they fall under the 'too-soon-old, too-late-smart category'. While we share common problems as we age, we experience them individually and, in addition, it is likely that each of us will have conditions or circumstances that are uniquely our own.

I have found that coordinated mechanics are, for me at least, the linchpin that makes singing possible. As teachers, we all begin with posture and alignment with our beginning students, and rightly so. My interest in that prompted me to pose in a number of common positions with postural faults as well as examples of the best I could do, to show my voice class. (These photos at least attest to my long-standing interest, though had I known I was going to use them for this chapter, I would not have used the silly hats.) I have included a current "best I can do photo."

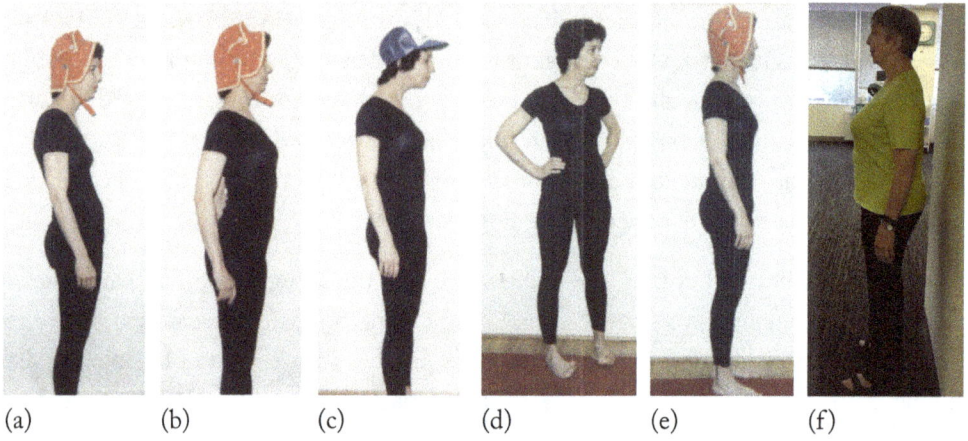

Figure 6.1 (a) Basic slouch; (b) Arched back; (c) Forward head position; (d) Supinated feet; (e) My prior best; (f) My current best

For every inch of forward head position, ten pounds of weight are added, according to Kapandji (*Physiology of Joints*, Vol. 3). Initially, my interest was due to how alignment affected breathing and just to have good posture. Later, my interest deepened to wondering how posture affected all the muscles that position the larynx in the throat. I studied Alexander Technique and yoga, but I must confess that as the years passed, I was better at preaching good posture than I was at practicing it. Bifocals, time at the computer, fatigue, and concentration on taking care of family members and others led to forward head position and slumping. Looking at the extrinsic laryngeal muscles in an anatomy book such as Zemlin's, one can imagine how the shortening of one and the lengthening of another would affect function and yet all of these work together in complex ways, so it's almost impossible to isolate them. Linda Spencer, speech language pathologist, once said, "Muscles are party animals, they like to go places in groups."

About 8 years ago, rather suddenly, I found that I could no longer sing easily above the staff, and I often felt as if a muscle spasm was imminent. (In retrospect, this might have been muscular tension dysphonia (MTD), but that was not diagnosed, though mild reflux was addressed.) I now could relate to some of my older students in ways that I could not before. I felt that if I could solve this for myself, it would help me help my students, particularly those over age fifty. During this time, I dutifully went to work with my coach, Gillian Cookson, every week and we read through music that I was considering for my students, worked out ornamentation for them, and discussed repertoire. I am eternally grateful that she stuck with me, allowed me to flip octaves and not work to prepare recital programs. I used less demonstration and more description in my teaching.

Quite by accident, through a student with Bell's palsy, I met Jodi Barth, a physical therapist and her assistant, Gincy Stezar, who specialize in MTD and facial palsy. I initially went to see them, calendar in hand, to ask if they would come to speak to my voice pedagogy class. Before Jodi even considered that, she said, "But look at you!" The next thing I knew, my shoes were off, I was fitted with orthotics, my shoulders were taped with kinesiotape, and exercises were prescribed. Only then did we look at the calendar and they agreed to come and speak to my class. I felt that I had stumbled into a resource for solving problems and had found a missing piece of the vocal puzzle. I added physical therapist to the voice care team of laryngologist, speech language pathologist, teacher, coach, and Alexander Technique or movement teacher.

Since each singer is different, I urge you to find a physical therapist who is as specialized as Jodi and who understands singers to get your own specific stretching and strengthening exercises, but I will describe the ones that helped me and the ways in which I tailored them to my needs. I also believe that yoga, Feldenkrais, and Alexander Technique are valuable, especially in maintaining good habits and usage. Alexander Technique teachers maintain "it's not posture, but a movement," and I agree, so my use of the term "posture" does not imply a locked position. Physical therapy offers specific remedies that zero in on problems and makes the other approaches more effective. It is also true that doing exercises for 15 minutes and then spending the next two hours hunched over the computer is NOT going to address the problems.

Since my twenties, I have carried tension in my right shoulder in a knot that could sometimes cause tingling that would travel up my neck. Tension in the trapezius is a common problem, and only with these basic exercises, which no one had suggested before, did the knot go away in my case. Let your physical therapist guide you. Using the following exercises, in about a year and a half, I felt I was back to my normal, aging self and used my usual vocalises to warm up the voice.

Basic Thera-Band® (brand of resistance latex band) exercises

1. Holding the Thera-Band, palms up, elbows bent and close to the body, squeeze shoulder blades together and spread hands apart, as if pulling out your pockets and saying that you have no money. (With Jodi Barth, Center for Facial Recovery.)

Figure 6.2 Exercise 1 using a Thera-Band®

2. Anchor the Thera-Band to a solid object. (I have iron grid work where it is always hanging. In a hotel, you can knot the band or loop a towel around it and toss the towel over a door and close it.) With the Thera-Band attached at a level taller than your head, grasp the band, arms straight and pull it to shoulder level. It is important to squeeze the base of the shoulder blades together. (With Gincy Stezar, Center for Facial Recovery)

Figure 6.3 Exercise 2 using a Thera-Band®

3. With the Thera-Band anchored at waist level, grasp it as if picking up a suitcase and with arms straight, pull hands behind you to a comfortable distance. Again, squeeze the base of the shoulder blades together. **It is not about the arms**.

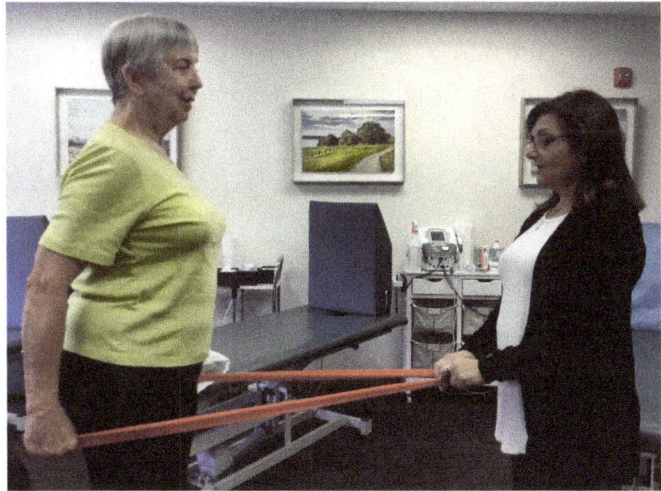

Figure 6.4 Exercise 3 using a Thera-Band®

When I do these three exercises, the knot in my shoulder goes away. If I don't do them, my shoulder talks to me with tension and pain. I do them once a day in three repetitions of ten for each.

Other common stretches

1. Put one bent arm behind the back, tip your head to the opposite side, ear to shoulder and use that hand on your head, not to pull, but to use the weight of that to increase the stretch. Do three times each side (unless advised otherwise) and hold for a count of thirty.

2. Turn head to the side, going as far over the shoulder as is comfortable. This is a good one for the car at long stoplights.

3. Lying on the floor, tuck the chin in slightly to stretch the back of the neck. Do it up to ten times holding for a count of five to ten. Another good one for the car, pressing back of the head into the head rest. Do not tip the head back, go straight back. Jodi introduced me to the importance of the longus capitis and longus colli, deep muscles of the neck, scarcely mentioned in the speech anatomy books.

More specific to me

Many years ago, we used to do head rotations, swinging the head back as well as in front. The current thinking is not to do that, and I was very careful to simply bend head to ear, roll to the front and then take head to the other ear. Jodi pointed out that I was tight in the front of my throat and the only way to stretch that was to tip my head back a bit, and protrude my jaw slightly, as a man might in shaving. A la Alexander, I was to tip at the top of my neck, the occipital joint, with my hands on my chest to encourage it to stay stable.

My adaptation

Firmly sliding the skin of my sternum downward, I found that it was uncomfortable to swallow. Consequently, I do this downward slide with my fingers while vocalizing to signal the constrictor (swallowing) muscles to remain inactive as I go into the top of my voice. We have more elevators of the larynx than we have depressors, and they are sneaky, activating without our awareness. (The top two constrictors start the food down the throat, but the inferior constrictor elevates the larynx. If you have ever needed to speak just as you were swallowing, you have noticed what a squawk you produced!)

There is a yoga posture in which you exhale and then, with vocal folds closed, act as if you are inhaling. This gives you a passive tracheal pull, lowering the larynx more than when you are inhaling. It has been posited that this increases the space between the hyoid and the thyroid, but I suspect that it simply lowers both, but it's a nice downward stretch.

Jaw equalizer

Insert your index fingers on each side of your mouth, between your teeth, straight back. Bite down gently. Do you feel equal contact and pressure on both sides? If not, try to equalize it. The effect lasts as long as it lasts, but better is better! This is a good one to do in the shower as your hands are clean and you don't need gloves.

Jaw stabilizer

Putting the tongue to the roof of the mouth, tongue tip sliding toward the soft palate, open and close the jaw slowly. You will probably find that the clicking and grinding sounds disappear. Jodi Barth calls such exercises "neuromuscular re-education."

My adaptation

I put my tongue in this position and do glides, stopping when I feel any pulling or strain. I always follow this with some tongue stretches outside the mouth to return the tongue to a neutral position. (You may have noticed that Domingo's tongue goes up when he sings high notes, he himself spoke of that in Jerome Hines' book, *Great Singers on Great Singing*, and he used a mirror in recording sessions; his career has lasted for decades.)

Using my work with Jodi, I have experimented in other ways. Using the second knuckle of my index finger, I explore any tender spots on my chin -if I find one, I massage it firmly. I then go under my chin, right next to the bone. Because I carry my tension in my right shoulder, I often find more tension under my jaw on the right side, so I protrude my jaw slightly and stroke from my chin to my hyoid bone. Take care not to press on lymph nodes or the thyroid gland, I'm told that glands do not like to be poked!

One day Jodi and Gincy came by my studio and I had crossed legs at the piano. Jodi asked if I often did that and I had to say yes, especially when I am tired. She gave me hip flexor exercises and I no longer was prompted to cross my legs. When I don't do the stretches, I find the legs wanting to cross because one "sit bone" does not meet the bench.

Hip flexor stretch

Lie on your back with legs hanging off the edge of the bed with bent knees. Pull right knee up to the chest and leave the other thigh flat on the bed to avoid arching the back. Hold for 30 seconds. Follow your physical therapist's advice on whether to do both sides. There is a more advanced version of this, but this is a good beginning exercise.

Breath

Zemlin says that residual breath (the air that we cannot exhale) doubles between the ages of 20 and 79, as we lose compliance, so most of us find that we can't expel as much air as we used to. That means that the more compliance and flexibility we can preserve, the better we are able to "spend our air" and sustain the long phrases. This also means that the buoyant rib cage is able to recover and take in air on the inhalation between phrases more efficiently. Again, posture and body position! Of course, we may need to program an extra breath in a long phrase, no harm done.

Unique challenge

I have rather impressive tori (torus, singular); these are bony outgrowths on the roof of the mouth. My tori begin at the gum line and almost completely fill my palatal arch. Young people can get them, too, but the elderly are more likely to have them. I feel the effects on my articulation and find that I am more sluggish when I am tired or not well hydrated. In addition to rest and hydration, paying attention to tongue stretches helps keep articulation from sounding "old."

Noisy brain

Noisy brain is the term Norman Doidge uses in *The Brain's Way of Healing* to describe the irregular firing of neurons in old age. "… the suprachiasmatic nucleus (SCN) regulates our biological clock. …the organ clock, like an old watch, no longer keeps good time." (p.119–120) Most of us find that it is harder to memorize music as we get older; it takes longer to get it to "stick." Mindfulness as we practice it, both mentally and physically, is an important skill and we benefit from putting that into play. "Use it or lose it" and "Rest and rust," are clichés that have stood the test of time. I highly recommend this book.

Unmet challenge

There is a loss of power in the bottom fifth of my voice and I hear that in other older singers as well. Loss of breath power and tissue changes in the vocal folds may be responsible, but I hypothesize that, in the absence of vocal fold bowing, it may be partly a matter of conditioning. I have not spent enough time singing in that lower range to test my hypothesis, but it would make an interesting study.

For the past 25 years, I have believed that studying articulation and the role the strap muscles play in positioning the larynx in the throat are the last frontier in voice research. At least, it seems to have been given scant attention, though to be sure, just when we think we have learned everything about breathing, for example, we find that we need to look at it again.

I have always tried to teach using fact-based pedagogy, and I still do, even when I use imagery to get the desired result. I get impatient, cranky even, when others pat the tummy and call it the diaphragm, or "smell the rose" to lift the palate. That said, I have to admit that as I have worked with my aging self, I have found some exercises helpful that I cannot explain with "facts." I have comforted myself with thoughts of people like Feldenkrais: he had an injured knee, but noticed that when he injured his good leg, he could stand on the bad one (Doidge, p.164). A number of discoveries about the functioning of the brain/body connection have begun with "noticing." I think what I have suggested could be tested and I welcome others to do so. In fact, I still hope to do that myself; perhaps my dream as a young singer of taking part in laboratory experiments and study will still be realized. I have tried some of these approaches with younger students and found them to be helpful.

I must confess that I have not always been a model participant in my own neuro-muscular re-education. When my schedule has gotten too hectic, I have allowed myself to be lax in the work I need to do, and I have paid the price. From time to time, I need to see Jodi and Gincy for a remedial "jumpstart." In addition to the kinesiotape, Jodi has become certified in dry needling and uses it to release tight muscles and that can be dramatic. She and Gincy also use cupping, gentler than what was in evidence in the Olympic swimmers in 2014, and low-level laser. Both Jodi and Gincy have worked inside my mouth to release tensions and improve my jaw alignment. If a muscle is knotted with non-functioning tension, these techniques can facilitate a return to the maintenance regimen that keeps the body functioning at its new normal optimal level. My advice: stay with it!

We have a number of glorious singers past the age of fifty: Renée Fleming, Susan Graham, Frederica Von Stade, the indefatigable Placido Domingo, of course, and the beloved Barbara Cook, who just recently passed away. Five years ago, my colleague Linda Mabbs gave a magnificent performance as Miss Havisham in Argento's *Miss Havisham's Fire*, and Carmen Balthrop has earned the title of Mama Diva from former students, deservedly so. I applaud them madly both for the performances and for the discipline it took to schedule life and lessons in a way that allowed them to perform at that level.

Will there be another performance in my future? Perhaps. Gillian Cookson has told me that I really should give another recital. I thought about calling one Sing a Song of Seventy, and that year passed, and then another … She says that I could call it Still Alive at Seventy-Five, or Still Got Kicks at Seventy-Six, or Seventy-Seven Could be Heaven! It takes more discipline and concentration now, but that's a good thing. Even singers at their peak can have an off night, and that is certainly possible as a senior singer, so the risk is a known factor.

What about you?

Do you really want to sing? Sometimes singing makes us feel better and lifts our spirits, but the voice feels creaky and scratchy – don't let that stop you! Can you hum or sigh? Swing your arms? Sing with the masking sound of a vacuum cleaner while cleaning? This tends to make us less judgmental and keeps us moving. Make a start with short vocalizing sessions and then gradually lengthen them. Choose songs that are comfortable.

Do you have something to say? Maybe we don't have the bloom of youth, but we have a deeper understanding of our message and that understanding results in a compelling performance. In a master class that I attended at the Kennedy Center, Barbara Cook said, "It's hard to believe, whatever you're doing, that you're enough. We are all, always, enough."

If you want to sing and express yourself, become your own lab experiment and follow your best trial balloons – that is, if a particular vocalization feels good, keep doing it. You will not get any younger, and yet, right now, you are the youngest you will ever be. What are you waiting for?

Suggested reading (in addition to the standard pedagogy texts)

Books

Coyle, Daniel (2009) *The Talent Code* New York, NY: Bantam Dell.
Denes, Peter B., and Elliot N. Pinson (1973) *The Speech Chain: The Physics and Biology of Spoken Language* Garden City, NY: Anchor Books.
Doidge, Norman (2007) *The Brain That Changes Itself* New York, NY: Penguin Books.
Doidge, Norman (2015) *The Brain's Way of Healing* New York, NY: Penguin Books.
Doscher, Barbara (1994) *The Functional Unity of the Singing Voice* Boulder, C0: Scarecrow Press.

Duhigg, Charles (2012) *The Power of Habit: Why We Do What We Do in Life and Business* New York, NY: Random House.

Feldenkrais, Moshe (1972, 1977) *Awareness through Movement* New York, NY: Harper & Row.

Gelb, Michael (1981) *Body Learning: An Introduction to the Alexander Technique.* New York, NY: Delilah Books.

Graaff, Kent M. Van de, and Stuart Ira Fox (1989) *Concepts of Human Anatomy and Physiology* Dubuque, IA: W.C. Brown Publishers.

Gray, Henry, F.R.S. (1974) *Gray's Anatomy* Philadelphia, PA: Running Press.

Kendall, Florence Peterson, Elizabeth Kendall McCreary, Patricia Geise Provance et al. (2005) *Muscles: Testing and Function with Posture and Pain* 5ed, Baltimore, MD: Lippincott Williams & Wilkins.

Levitin, Daniel J. (2006) *This is Your Brain on Music* New York, NY: Plume, Published by Penguin Group.

Levitin, Daniel J. (2008) *The World in Six Songs: How the Musical Brain Created Human Nature* New York, NY: Dutton, published by Penguin Group.

McCoy, Scott. *Your Voice: An Inside View* (2012) Delaware, OH: Inside View Press.

Sacks, Oliver (2008) *Musicophilia*, New York, NY: Borzoi, published by Alfred A. Knopf.

Sataloff, Robert T. (2017) *Vocal Health and Pedagogy: Advanced Assessment and Treatment* 3ed. San Diego, CA: Plural Publishing Inc.

Schwiebert, Jerald, with Candace Platt (2012). *Physical Expression and the Performing Artist: Moving beyond the Plateau.* Ann Arbor, MI: The University of Michigan Press.

Titze, Ingo R. (1994) *The Principles of Voice Production.* Englewood Cliffs, NJ.: Prentice Hall.

Zemlin, Willard R. (1988) *Speech and Hearing Science*, 3ed. Englewood Cliffs, NJ: Prentice Hall.

Journals

Schneider, Carole M., Carolyn A. Dennehy, and Keith G. Saxo (1997) Exercise Physiology Principles Applied to Vocal Performance: The Improvement of Postural Alignment *Journal of Voice* 11(3): 332–337.

Staes, Fillip F., Lieve Jansen, Ann Vilette et al. (2011) Physical Therapy as a Means to Optimize Posture and Voice Parameters in Student Classical Singers: A Case Report. *Journal of Voice* 25(3): 91–101.

8

Aging, HRT, and stabilizing the voice

Lisa Popeil

What is easier, what is more challenging about working with older students?

The easiest aspect of working with older singing students is their lack of expectation. In my studio, most over-50s sing for pleasure or to present at a low-key family or church event. They're happy with any improvement in control, range, or tone they can achieve and realize that learning the techniques of expression and interpretation may be more accessible and useful than technical perfection in their quest for self-expression and joy in singing.

What can be challenging for me, in terms of creating a game plan, is that older singers generally lack the drive for excellence that I see in my younger students. The over-50s come to me with curiosity or a desire to fix a technical issue, but rarely have the passion or commitment to think long-term about how fabulous a singer they may still become. This attitude is not surprising really, but still I think many over-50s shortchange themselves and give up too easily or imagine that, as much as they enjoy singing, what's the use in continuing if there's no potential career ahead.

What are typical medical questions you are asked by men and women?

By far, the most common medical problem is reflux. Recently, at least a third of new students over the age of twenty-five coming to me have had problems with hoarseness, fatigue and discomfort in the vocal folds. I experienced serious reflux problems from what I believe was lower estrogen during pre-menopause and experimented quite a bit, so I know what reflux-created hoarseness feels like. The good news is that there are several strategies available which work quickly and well, and my students notice improvement after about five days. I tell them that reflux, whether GERD or Laryngopharyngeal Reflux (LPR) is to be managed, not cured. Simply not drinking a big glass of water before bed has produced great results.

Allergies are a big problem in Southern California. It seems to be the price we pay for year-round foliage. Also, in the fall we get the Santa Ana winds with really low humidity, as low as 10%, which wreaks havoc on vocal fold tissue. Singers' vocal folds can sound like "dried leaves" when it gets super dry. For that, I have them use my Omron nebulizer with saline for a few minutes. It helps plump up their folds, restores their ability to sing high notes and creates a smooth, glossy, easy sound.

What do your students say they are experiencing with their voice?

Interestingly, new amateur students don't usually say much. I don't think they know enough about the terminology of vocal technique to specify what they may need. They just want a professional ear to help them sing better. Professional singers usually, but not always, have a clearer idea of what they want to work on, such as vibrato, knowing their range, learning how to support or wanting to try a new style. For my older students at their first lesson, I liken the experience to going to a doctor's office for a quick review of all aspects of their vocal technique or vocal health issues. And then we fix.

Have you noticed a difference between the changes experienced by long-term students, or challenges found with newcomers? Or with people who have sung in choirs for a length of time, or sung solo?

I haven't. And everyone is so different. Some experienced singers are in really bad shape with long-standing habits and then there are the occasional singers who are really quite good and are surprised when I let them know how well they sing. Choir singers can have a challenging time transiting to the rhythmic and melodic freedom required of commercial styles, especially moving to jazz. They want to sing the note as it is on the page and any other way seems plain wrong!

What individual experiences have you noticed or been told about with those who chose hormone replacement or decided against it?

When I hit menopause at 52, I decided I wasn't going to do it. I didn't know what that meant exactly but I researched and found a radical and little-known method of bio-identical hormone replacement called the Schwarzbein Protocol. I found several trained practitioners in Southern California who I've been working with for the last eight years and have been very happy with the results. It's not for every woman, since the protocol produces a monthly period, indefinitely, but if I can trick my brain into thinking I'm forty-five and fertile and worth keeping around, I'm on board.

The only older female student who had serious post-menopausal vocal changes was a lady who said that, when younger, she had been a coloratura soprano and that after menopause, lost one and a half octaves off her high notes. But instead of being depressed about it, she said (with a big smile) "It's fine, now I get to sing jazz!" Otherwise, I rarely notice any vocal problems related to age in my older students aside from typical problems usually related to lack of abdominal breath support.

What differences in breath do you see after the fifth decade?

I'm a strong believer that clear, precise and reliable abdominal breath support is the missing ingredient in vocal pedagogy in general and even though under-support or incorrect support is heard in young singers of course, older singers often don't compensate as much as the young. Therefore, older singers may exhibit less "compensatory tension", such as neck, jaw and tongue tension than younger singers but don't have enough 'oomph' to get the vocal folds to vibrate in a solid and consistent way. The over-50s may be more relaxed when singing and not adequately engaged physically, resulting in a weaker sound with less ability to sing high or loudly.

What exercises do you use specifically for breath?

First, I think it's important that singers and teachers separate the terms "breathing" and "support" in their minds and bodies. Calling any breath function, in or out, as "breathing" can lead to vocal issues in singers because it's confusing. I've found it useful to teach that "breathing" is the action of bringing air into the lungs and "support" is the action of the torso and abdomen which pressurizes the outgoing air controlling vocal fold vibration. Put another way, breathing is what you do when you're NOT singing, and support is what you do when you ARE singing.

After decades of experimentation, I teach four jobs of support for singing:

1. Upper chest stays up with no dropping during singing,
2. side and back ribs remain slightly wide during singing with no collapsing,
3. the upper belly "magic spot" (below the sternum) should firm OUT like a spongy wall for every sung note, and
4. the lower belly (the navel and several inches below) should clutch IN for singing.

For breathing, meaning air intake, I believe that the chest should stay comfortably elevated but not rise and the ribcage should remain comfortably wide. Both the upper and lower bellies should relax, air coming into the lungs using the body's natural vacuum function, and finally to feel satisfied, one can gently and silently "fill", imaging that air coming into the lower belly then rising up to the top of the head. So, exhale on "hoo", RELEASE (bellies), FILL. Repeat.

There are many alternate ways to teach breathing and support, but I've found that this method works for all styles of singing, all bodies and is easily learned. So again, support for singing, release for breathing with no "inhaling", shoulder lifting, chest raising or noisy intake sounds, unless of course a noisy intake sound is an artistic choice.

My go-to exercises for support are the "SH Pattern". With 2–3 fingers on the upper belly "magic spot" (the spot or region below the sternum which goes out the MOST when making a loud "SH" sound) and thumb on the navel and the rest of that hand's fingers just below, the singer makes a very loud "SH" sound. Upper belly goes OUT, lower belly goes IN. Then for breathing, open mouth, open vocal folds, release both upper and lower belly, feel air come in quietly, then fill with air silently.

The timing for the "SH" pattern is as follows: "SH" loudly for one second, release for air intake for one second. Repeat four times total. (This is what I call the short portion). Then hold the "SH" very loudly for four seconds, then release for two seconds. (This is the long portion.)

"SH" PATTERN

SH, release, SH, release, SH, release, SH, release, SH>>>1, 2, 3, off on 4, release

When doing this exercise, there should be no discernible movement of the chest or ribs. Also, it's important to try to crescendo on the long portion rather than have the pressure (and volume) fade at the end of the four seconds.

This exercise not only separates and coordinates the breathing and support functions, but it builds muscle strength as well.

What do you find stabilizes the voice or destabilizes it?

Though I feel that increasing abdominal and thoracic support is the main stabilizer of the voice, I also have found that the jaw is surprisingly effective in stabilizing excessive laryngeal movement, such as in the case of a wobbly vibrato. Classical vocal pedagogy treasures singing with a loose jaw, but with age, that looseness can lead to lack of stabilization of the larynx. In addition, as the thyroid-cricoid joint ossifies over time, there's a possibility that the thyroid/cricoid visoring action typical of many vibratos is unable to occur resulting in a larger laryngeal movement with every vibrato cycle. Hence, the wobble.

Engaging the masseter muscle firms the lower jaw somewhat, while still allowing for freedom of movement. And this action allows older singers the possibility of increasing the speed of their vibratos. The keywords for this kind of jaw action are "firm but flexible". I also use a hand gesture I call "vibrato fingers" which can be instantly effective in speeding up a too-slow vibrato.

Vibrato Fingers

Place flat hand in front of face, palm down, thumb towards nose. The other hand (2-3 fingers) can be used to monitor that the upper belly "magic spot" is engaged "out and firm". Then start with a well-supported straight tone on an "ee" vowel, medium volume. Initiate vibrato and wiggle fingers away from face while keeping magic spot out. Most singers, of any age, should notice that their vibrato is now faster, even and in control.

I've found that most singers who have vibrato problems have straight tone problems as well. So we make sure the straight tone is solid, with no pressing of the vocal folds and no shakiness at all before we move on to perfecting vibrato.

It's fun to explain that vibrato is a mechanical motion of the larynx, "wiggling". Knowing that vibrato is a 'feel-able', controllable action can be quite reassuring to any singer.

What exercises/vocalises do you use that help with range extension?

To determine one's absolute low note, I like to use the "aw" vowel with a dropped chin and a "fishy" mouth shape on the pattern 54321 at a soft volume with straight tone. Then we descend in semi-tones until the lowest note is heard:

AW 54321 to determine lowest notes

For high notes, my favorite is the lip trill with one hand monitoring the lower belly support. The lower belly support acts as a "high note helper" and should go in **more** as the pitches ascend. The pattern I use is:

Lip Trill to determine highest notes:1358 with staccato on the last note

If there's any difficulty accessing the very highest notes of the range, I suggest the "Point Over". Take a single hand and point "up and over" for the highest notes. You point upwards, raising a shoulder and then lean forward pointing towards the floor while doing the lip trill (or tongue trill, as an alternate). This action enables the thyroid cartilage tilting-down function used in pitch-raising for highest head voice pitches.

Pointing up and over while doing the lip or tongue trill 1358 pattern above

In Los Angeles, most women over 50 with whom I work are on some kind of hormone replacement, often bio-identical hormones. None of my male students supplement with hormones, as far as I know. I even had a 92-year old female singer who looked stunning and sang remarkably well in a cabaret style.

Whether taking hormone replacement or not, I encourage all my singers to stretch regularly, (my favorites being Yoga and Pilates), maintaining a good weight, not letting oneself go over time and to regularly sing throughout the length of their range with sirens, hums or lip/tongue trills.

I also believe that maintaining muscle strength throughout the body is vital to keeping the voice pliable and reliable, so I also suggest weight-lifting.

9

Hearing, sliding pitch, wobble, and hitting the gravel

Martha Howe

As with all age-related changes, there are several culprits for both sliding pitch and developing a wobble. Some specific causes are changes in the neuromuscular reactivity, both in the larynx and throughout the body, meaning that the muscles in your body are not responding as well or as quickly to the messages being sent by the nerves. The physical coordination involved in producing a pitch is quite complicated, so if the nerves and muscles aren't communicating as well as they were, there can be problems in the pitch itself, and in the quality of sound. Add to this that the vocal folds may not be closing as well as they were because of laryngeal tension, compensatory tension in the tongue, jaw, and neck, and the probability of uneven breath flow.

Compromised hearing is another one of the major players in both sliding pitch and wobble. The hearing loss common to aging is called presbycusis, and can go unnoticed because it is a gradual, slow process affecting both ears. It affects high-frequencies, making it tricky to differentiate between 'b', 'p', and 't'. Early signs are difficulty understanding speech in noisy or screechy environments.

Hearing loss in general can be more pronounced in singers and voice teachers as well as all voice professionals working in consistently noisy environments. On stage, what can look like an affectionate gesture as the tenor cups the soprano's face, is actually protection as he covers her ears during his high notes. But ensembles and scenes are not always so easily controlled. Singing Maddalena in a *Rigoletto* I turned the wrong way and caught one of the tenor's B flats directly in my ear. My ear buzzed at B flat for years afterwards. Actors must deal with shouting, fight scenes, and stage-effects noises like gunshots.

It has been determined that sound levels above 85 decibels can do damage, and enthusiastic choirs can produce 90 decibels and above, with peaks over 100 decibels. Imagine an opera ensemble and chorus in full flight, or long rehearsals in acoustically bright rooms, or standing on stage with an orchestra for a large choral work and chorus members who feel the need to out-shout the orchestra. Then there are festive and special religious services when brass and percussion can be wedged in behind the choir for those triumphant moments that leave your ears ringing for days.

Sirens, screeching train wheels and subway cars, hockey and ball games, loud bars, clubs, and dances, as well as pumped-up karaoke speakers can do damage, along with unexpected, sudden microphone feedback, and concerts where the amplified sound is raised incrementally to rock-stadium levels. These are all detrimental to your hearing. So is spending hours in an enclosed room with singers who are enjoying new-found volume, especially in their upper range. Taking all of these together, it is easy to understand how actors, choral singers, soloists, and teachers are prone to high-frequency hearing loss and speech-frequency hearing loss. There are also ototoxic medications to be careful with, which include large quantities of aspirin (the salicylates), chemotherapy treatments, and aminoglycoside antibiotics.

Hearing-aid research has found that when the ears are not sending a particular signal to the brain, the brain stops 'listening' for it, and there is diminished neural connectivity. They recommend correcting a loss earlier rather than later, when it may be too late for the brain to fully process it any more.

And remember, the voice you hear in your head is **not** what is heard in the room. That includes pitch, which can be affected by how aerobic and steady your exhalation is, vibrato, vowel clarity, mouth shape, and jaw, neck and tongue tension. It is easy to get lazy and assume you are on pitch because you are generally matching pitch inside your head. Each pitch has a treble and bass component. The treble part of a voiced/sung pitch is directional and travels forward from your mouth, with only a very small part reaching back to your ears. Inside your head, even less of the treble portion reaches your inner ear. Meanwhile, the bass portion dominates the hearing from both your inner and outer ear. What does that mean? At best you are hearing only a small portion of your real sound.

Sound check: Place your hands on your face, thumbs near your ears. Now move them out an inch or so from your face, speak, pivoting your hands to find the sweet zone where you are sending more of your true voice bouncing from your palms back to your ears. (Generally, your fingertips will be canted toward your ears.)

Choir folders: You can bounce your voice back to yourself using your folder, held in front of you and slightly lower, at a shallow angle to your face. This is useful when you are insecure about a pitch and want to check what you are singing. But be aware that if you are sending the sound back to yourself, it's not going out front to the listeners.

Just as you are probably more attentive going down a steep staircase than you were in your twenties, now you need to listen more consciously and attentively. The feedback loop for pitch is **hearing**. That sounds self-evident, but conscious listening involves taking the sound inside of you, then demanding that your voice match that pitch and listening in the room to make sure that you are in tune with the other singers and the accompaniment.

Add to this the fact that many people hear a slight change in pitch when a tone gets louder. So, they may believe that they or their fellow singers have gone sharp or flat in a *forte* passage and try and compensate. We all hear differently, and how well we hear changes over time. Many a singer is led astray because they believe they know their melody and they stop listening carefully, mindfully, to the group or the accompaniment.

Addressing different pitch problems

This is a good time to use the voice memo app on your smartphone or the recording device of your choosing:

- Choose a favorite melody, something easy and mid-range, and record yourself singing it without accompaniment. How did you do?

- On YouTube, find a karaoke version of a song you enjoy and sing along. Record that, so you can see how you are doing with accompaniment.

- If you are consistently on pitch, well done! If not, don't be discouraged, and don't believe your apocalyptic inner critic.

- If it is the beginning or the end of the phrase that sags, it is probably a result of breath management. Sagging comes from being distracted, having low energy, and/or lazy, non-aerobic breath flow. We all tend to forget about our airflow during the second half of a phrase or during a long-held note, so the pitch sags. It's like taking your foot off the gas pedal and expecting the car to keep steadily climbing a hill. It doesn't work that way.

- Scooping into the first notes of the phrase can be remedied by clearly thinking the pitch before singing and releasing a bit of air through your nose or mouth to get the flow started.

- Overshooting (going sharp) on the beginning of a phrase or on a higher note could be from pushing too much air at the tone. The glottis is where the air goes over the vocal folds, and 'subglottal pressure' is the force of the air being sent over the vocal folds. Our bodies know exactly how much pressure is needed to make the vocal folds vibrate for a pitch, but often in attempting to 'support', we slam air at the glottis. This sudden increase in subglottal pressure will make a voice louder and can push pitch up as much as two semi-tones.

- Is the pitch sliding in the upper passaggio (upper third of the staff for most voices)? This area is particularly tricky for older voices because of a combination of all of the above. Habits and coping mechanisms from earlier decades don't work as well any more. There is a tendency to 'guesstimate' pitches from memory rather than consciously listen in the moment, and there is a need to make sure that air is flowing freely without muscling or pushing it.

Another possible culprit for both sliding pitch and wobble, is what's going on in your breath. You want as little jaw and tongue tension as possible in both your inhalation and your exhalation, with your shoulders relaxed and your chest open. There are many wonderful exercises to work on posture, and it is wise to tailor them to your personal physical structure and health. To 'open' the chest, think of your shoulder blades sliding 'down' your back (not pinching them together, which causes neck tension). There is a beautiful yogic description that the shoulder blades slide down your back 'to cradle your heart'.

There is a great deal of information about breathing, much of it contradictory. Obviously, it is controlled by our autonomic/involuntary control system, ticking along without our attention and keeping us alive. Then when it is time to sing, many people believe we should manipulate air and muscles, other people believe that if you find a sound that works then the correct breath will follow. I'm of the opinion that our bodies know how to breathe, but that singing and speaking are often done when our bodies are sitting or standing, so the breath is doing its minimum/resting thing. If we are moving around or dancing, then the body attunes the breath to the movement, rather than the voice. Healthy singing and presentational speaking require active, aerobic breathing to keep the air flowing. If the air isn't flowing easily, then the body uses other coping mechanisms to sustain the sound, which usually involve unwanted tension.

Pay attention to what is going on in your ribs when you breathe and when you sing. Some of our problems with sliding pitch and wobble come from slack muscles in our back and around the sides of our ribs. Your inhalation should be able to gently move and expand your ribs, so they open to the side, giving the lungs more room to expand.

Notice I said 'side' not front. (Think of horses who breathe in when the girth on their saddle is tightened. If it's not re-tightened after exhalation, then the saddle will be too loose and will slide around, dumping a surprised rider.) Another way to think of it is that your bronchi and lungs hang from the larynx. When you activate the muscles around the ribs it lifts some of the weight of that whole breathing apparatus and the larynx and throat aren't having to carry the whole load. How does your body feel when you are about to dance or play tennis? Now how does it feel when you are standing, waiting in line at the grocery store? Pay close attention to your body and see if you can feel the difference.

We can often think that good support involves energetically pushing air with your stomach muscles. But this can overload the glottis, often causing too much pressure at the beginning of a phrase and not leaving enough air for the end of a phrase. It can also give you an uneven airflow that can push notes sharp at the beginning of a phrase (from too much subglottal pressure) and leave the end of the phrase to sag a little flat (because you ran out of breath). Plus, energetically pushing air at your throat can cause tension in your throat and tongue, which can push a vibrato over the border to wobble.

Of course, your stomach muscles are involved in breathing, but they are not the whole story. Taking your attention to your ribs and imagining that you are breathing into your heart activates the muscles around your ribs which will help with the flexibility and strength of your breathing.

Here are some suggestions to help identify and relieve jaw, tongue, and throat tension and too much subglottal pressure:

Subglottal pressure vs. moving air

One of the best ways to check whether your air is moving easily is if you can smoothly move from soft to loud to soft again (*messa di voce*):

- First, relax your jaw and soften your tongue, so there is a finger's-width of space between your back upper and lower molars.

- The /s/s in this exercise should be sung gently, without the front teeth closing. The lips remain soft, not pulled back, and the /s/ is made by air flowing between the teeth, not caught between closed teeth. Say 'secret' to feel closed teeth. 'Silent' or 'sibilant' should point you toward the more open /s/.

- The softer /s/s should help keep the air flowing. If you feel your lips flare open, you are using the harder /s/ and probably more pressure rather than flowing air.

- In an easy, mid-range, sing the following scale up and down, repeating it on incrementally higher then lower starting pitches. Notice where everything seems to flow easily, and where it gets caught or you feel any tension in your jaw, lips or tongue. Try and release the tension and get more air moving. Can you do a *messa di voce* on that final /so/?

- si si si si su su su so so < >
  1   2   3   4   5   4   3   2   1

If you can do a *messa di voce* on the final /so/, try and do one on the top /su/. You can also play with this exercise doing a larger *messa di voce* over more notes, or over the entire exercise. Have fun with it, noticing how these different tasks effect the free flow of your air. Notice if your lips flare or you suddenly have trouble slowly getting soft again. Those are signs of using more pressure than flowing air. Try to not go too fast. Stay aware of what your air is doing.

Jaw tension release – for teachers, actors, singers ... anyone who uses their voice

- Rub your hands together until they are warm, then place your palms on your jaw, fingers towards your ears, to warm and relax the jaw.

- Loosen the hinge of the jaw – where the jaw bone connects to the skull – and send in the thought, the impulse, to relax.

- Gently massage along your jaw, using your thumb to massage the underside of the jaw.

- Massage where the jaw curves up toward the ears, including the muscles around the bottom of your ears.

- Use a gentle chewing motion to help the jaw loosen and release tension.

- Feel the jaw hinge gently drop down, so that there is space between your upper and lower back molars. You can check if there is vertical space by sliding your tongue between the upper and lower back molars, first one side then the other. (Don't chew your tongue!)

- Once your jaw is relaxed and there is vertical space between the upper and lower back molars, take a simple, open-mouth, inhalation and feel it move your middle ribs.

- Breathe in to a count of four,

- Then exhale to a count of eight, keeping your mouth slightly open and your jaw relaxed.
- Repeat several times, watching the inhalation gently move your middle ribs, and keeping the jaw loose and relaxed.

Adding sound

- Use a loose, soft-tongued, non-resonant hum, like saying, "hmmmm, I don't know …"
- Take the gentle, mid-ribcage inhalation (practiced above) and start this 'hmmmm' on the exhalation, holding it as long as is comfortable, paying attention to where it vibrates.
- Let the 'hmmmm' start to circle up and down like a siren, starting midrange then circling down and up and around in widening circles.
- Pay attention to your loose jaw, soft tongue, and vertical space between the back molars. The sound should be more vibration than resonance. You are after ease and release from tension.
- Rather than going for mask-resonance, keep the sound loose and notice the vibration move around in your head and chest.
- Be mindful of your inhalation, that it moves the middle ribs, not your shoulders or head. You will notice that this inhalation is very heart-centered.
- You might need to repeat some very gentle 'chewing' motion to keep releasing tension.
- Less is more! Chew as though you are at a formal dinner at Downton Abbey with soft food, not tearing into a hamburger at the local diner!
- Now keeping the ease and vertical space, let the 'hmmm' become a spoken "Buh, Buh, Buh", keeping your lips soft and jaw relaxed. Move the speaking pitch up and down, maintaining the relaxation.
- Evolve to saying, "I'd like to go! I'd like to do that!" and let the tongue do all the work, keeping lips and jaw relaxed.
- Move on to the spoken or sung exercises of your choice, keeping a heart-centered inhalation and continuing to release jaw, tongue, and lip tension.

'Hitting the gravel' when you speak or sing

aka muscle tension dysphonia, intermittent dysphonia, and task-specific dystonia

Somewhere along the way, your voice went rogue. It has started catching on certain notes, or certain vowels, and it feels like your throat closes and simply won't let the sound out. Suddenly, what used to work doesn't work anymore. This gravelly sound can happen when you are attempting a word starting with a vowel or a glottal plosive, or when you are attempting to be soft or loud, or on certain pitches, or in the lower passaggio, which can become a mine-field for women.

This unexpected gravelly sound seems to come out of nowhere. Two of the age-related factors at play are a thickening of the cover of the vocal folds which can cause huskiness in the middle voice, and general dryness due to the atrophy of the mucus glands under and near your vocal folds. Both of these relate to a loss of flexibility, passaggio issues, and loss of range, along with the gravel.

What can be done about it? Not surprisingly, we are right back to jaw, throat, and tongue tension, along with airflow and the quality of your exhalation while speaking or singing. You are probably trying to support the problematic word or tone with the muscles in your throat and neck. This might have worked for you for decades, but now it doesn't, and it won't anymore. The bad news is that it is only going to get worse if you don't address the underlying cause. If you can, work with a Speech Language Pathologist (SLP) to get your speaking voice into a healthier place. This will also help your singing voice.

The good news is that with mindful practice you can smooth out the gravel. Start with the Subglottal pressure vs. moving air and jaw tension release exercise above. Then add 'Turtle breath', 'Call vs. shout', and 'Semi-occluded vocal tract' (SOVT) exercises, below.

It is not easy to shift ingrained habitual physical responses, even when they aren't working for us anymore. It helps to move slowly, being clear what you want to do that is different from what you have been doing.

Start by intentionally releasing tension in your jaw, neck, tongue, and throat between phrases. This is a feeling of getting back to neutral, like passing through neutral between gears with a stick-shift car. It is a bit counter-intuitive, as we tend to want to hold on to the energy from the previous phrase. But there is residual tension that can build up phrase to phrase and obstruct the very energy you want. A car doesn't drive in neutral, but must go through neutral between gears or there's a lot of grinding.

Releasing tension between phrases allows for the energy of the new phrase to come in unobstructed.

An interesting yogic breathing exercise is the 'Turtle breath'. This is especially useful as it strengthens and stretches the strap muscles of your throat, the area between the top of your spine and your skull, and releases tension in your jaw. It also helps activate your throat chakra.

Turtle breath

Pay attention to your neck, this should be soothing, not painful. Be mindful and don't push the stretches. Move at a speed comfortable for your neck and spine.

- Seated or standing, slowly look up, reaching for the ceiling with your chin as you inhale through your nose (like a turtle looking up).
- For an extra stretch of the strap muscles, once you are looking upward, you can pull your lower lip toward your upper lip.
- Slowly lower your chin and face, exhaling, like the turtle drawing back into its shell.
- Repeat for a total of seven Turtle breaths

Call vs. shout exercises

An effective way to avoid undue tension and pressure throughout the vocal instrument, is to learn the physical differences between calling and shouting. When you are feeding your pet, or have a treat for them, you generally call to them. When you notice they are about to destroy something, you generally shout at them. 'Call' uses more head voice and is more sing-song, tending to easily swoop in pitch because the onset is lighter, and the breath flows easily. 'Shout' tends to be more mid-to-lower voice and uses more pressure and tension with sudden bursts of air – more like barking. You can tell by my descriptors that 'shout' will not be that good for your voice, so we will focus on 'call' which can be a wonderful tool for warming-up:

Loosen things up

- Inhale easily through the nose, feeling the inhalation go to your heart, as though the lungs are massaging your heart.

- Let the exhalation become Om (pronounced ah-oh-ooo-mmmm) feeling the vibration in different parts of your head and body, especially buzzing between the ears and in the upper skull (pituitary area). Play around with the sound.
- Massage along your jaw line, under the chin, and at the joint where the jaw connects to the skull.
- Siren on an 'ng' as in sing or hung, with a slightly open mouth, relaxed jaw, lips, and tongue, while increasing the range of the siren. It is easier to start in the mid-range and do slow circles up and down.
- Imitate the sound made by a creaking door, both up and down, noticing that your jaw is loose and that the sound is higher in your head.
- Try different types of 'creaking' – very nasal, and more middle of the upper head. Notice the tension in the nasal creaking, the ease when you use upper head spaces.
- Where does the creaking with the least amount of tension sit inside your head? That one should also have the widest range up and down.

It has recently been noted that whereas it normally takes about four hundred repetitions to create a new pathway in the brain, so that you can easily repeat an action, it only takes ten to twenty repetitions when it is done with a sense of child's play. These two games were given to me by Vanessa Dinning, a wonderful actress, teacher, and dialect coach. They work well with groups and choirs as well as individually and for freeing up the speaking voice:

Bowling for vowels

- Stand up, miming holding a bowling ball. If you are in a group, have someone suggest a vowel, and someone else choose a consonant. (Examples: /pa/ /bu/ /lee/)
- Bend your knees, swinging the imaginary bowling ball getting ready to bowl (this gets the body and breath active)
- Take a good inhalation, and as you start the chosen consonant/vowel combo, 'release' the imaginary ball and sustain the vowel on that initial pitch as you 'watch' the ball go all the way down the bowling lane, pointing at the imaginary ball (this should take at least five or six beats)
- Sustaining the vowel, swoop up in pitch as you point up, describing a high arc overhead and back to yourself. Your voice should follow the smooth arc up and down that you are looking at and pointing out.

Softball vowels

- A similar exercise that goes the opposite direction. Have someone suggest a vowel, and someone else choose a consonant. (Examples: /ku/ /fa/ /mo/)

- Holding an imaginary softball, loosen your lower body getting 'ready' to throw the ball.

- Take a good inhalation, and as you start the chosen consonant vowel combo, 'throw' the ball and sustain the vowel as you swoop up in pitch, pointing up and over, describing a high arc away from and then back to you. Your voice should follow the smooth arc up and down that you are looking at and pointing out.

Having a greater sense of play will let adults relax into the fun of imitating a cuckoo clock, or a European police siren to find the feeling of 'call' high in the middle of your head. With individuals, it is helpful to have them experiment with the name of their pet or use a favorite endearment. This is a short list to give you some ideas:

- Cuckoo! Cuckoo!
- You-hoo! Honey!
- Mommy? Mommy? Mommy!
- Who-eee!
- Really? Really!
- Ogni or ogno

The magic of semi-occluded vocal tract exercises (SOVT)

In an over simplification, there is some heavy-duty math and science behind the idea that the 'semi-occlusion' or partial opening and closing of the mouth creates a back pressure that helps the vocal folds vibrate with more ease and less muscular effort. It literally squares up the vocal folds so that they will vibrate in a more even, healthy way.

SOVT exercises are wonderfully healthy for speaking as well as singing as they are helpful in getting your tongue, lips, and lower face to relax, and to get you more aware of the strength and consistency of your exhalation.

The following are a sampling of SOVT exercises, and can all be sustained without a specific pitch, or on a sustained pitch, or they can be used with the glides, sirens, or pitched exercises of your choice:

Fricatives: Using one of the voiced fricatives and prolonging the sound: /v/ /zh/ /z/ /th/ (as in 'them').

'Sh' finger to lips: Placing your index finger over your pursed lips while saying Shh-hhhhh.

Closed /u/ (ooo): Using a closed /u/ with 'kissy' lips.

Lip Trills: where the lips are relaxed and vibrating while you exhale. If you have trouble getting it started, Place your fingers on either side of the mouth, palms on your chin, little fingers on the outer edge of your mouth. Then exhale to set your lips trilling/ buzzing/ vibrating. Shift your hands around to find what works best to create the trill. You will notice that the buzz/trill stops if your exhalation is uneven or interrupted.

Raspberry: similar to the lip trill, but with the tongue out. You can do an upper lip raspberry, or a lower lip raspberry. Again, your exhalation must be strong and consistent to sustain the raspberry.

Tongue Trill: some English speakers have trouble with this as they are not used to sustaining a tongue trill. It can help to get the air flowing with an 'hrrrrr'. The tongue trill requires both flowing air and a relaxed tongue. When used with sirens and glides it will show you where you have unwanted tension in your tongue or jaw.

There is much information online about SOVT and straw phonation exercises and they are well-represented on YouTube. Ingo Titze has been a major proponent of straw phonation and SOVT work, and it is helpful to listen to his video, Vocal Straw Exercise (https://www.youtube.com/watch?v=0xYDvwvmBIM).

Straw Phonation: Speaking or singing through a straw, especially one that has the other end placed into a glass of water, not only lets your inner child come out to play, it shows you what your airflow is doing. You will feel if you are pushing too much air through, as the air will 'back up' into your mouth, and the water bubbles created by your voice provide direct feedback. If you don't want that feedback splashing all over you, only fill the container about a third full. You can also use water bottles or jars that help contain the splashing.

- Relax your jaw and tongue and be sure that your sound comes out the straw itself, not around the straw or through your nose.

- Keep your lips as calm as possible, closed around the straw, but ideally not tense or pursed.

- You will get a better result with the straw slightly on your tongue, not right at the lips.

- You should not feel like you are blowing through the straw, but rather like it is an extension of your vocal tract.

Straw phonation is like massaging your vocal folds and very good for seeing and feeling what is happening when you speak or sing. You can use straws with different diameters and see which feels the best for you. At the very least, SOVT exercises will ease the tension from too much speaking or singing and help your vocal folds get back into better synchronization. There are ecologically friendly straws to be found these days made out of bio-degradable materials, there are also metal straws to be kept and used over and over again, and there are devices such as those produced by companies like doctorVOX for Lax Vox Therapy or PhoRTE.

Lax Vox Therapy uses a tube in a closed container for the SOVT exercises. You can see the types of turbulence more clearly in an open container, which the scientists liked, but there was a lot of splashing. Lax Vox Therapy has produced several options available through doctorVOX:

- Lax Vox Tube: which is a simple silicone tube with a wide diameter (nine to twelve millimeters) that you put into a half-liter bottle of water that is half-full.

- pocketVOX: is very popular with professional voice users. It is a Y-shaped tube that screws onto the top of a standard half-liter water bottle. The longer tube is for SOVT phonation exercises and practicing, and the shorter tube can be used to hydrate your lungs by inhaling the humid air that is inside the bottle. The longer tube is even marked for the four different vocal tract lengths: youth, sopranos and tenors, mezzos and baritones, and altos and basses. You can cut it to the appropriate length for your voice-type. There are stoppers for the two tubes so it can be closed between uses and for traveling.

- doctorVOX: which is like the pocketVOX but more elaborate and intended for clinical use. It is made from glass and shaped so that the bubbling can be better monitored, and has a lanyard so you can wear it hands-free (and not drop it as often, I imagine). There is also a maskVOX which allows articulation and is good for working with dysphonia.

The Flow Ball is a simple and fun option for working on your exhalation and is especially good for those who respond to visual feedback. It looks rather like a toy plastic pipe, with a ping-pong ball in the pipe bowl. When you exhale or phonate/sing through the pipe, the airflow raises the ball so there is direct visual feedback on whether or not your air is flowing smoothly by how the ball reacts. There are several brands, but they differ in how the air is directed through the pipe, and the recommended brand is sold by The Voice Foundation through its online Store: voice-foundation.org

Phonatory Resistance Training Exercises (PhoRTE) is a research-based therapy program for Parkinson's and age-related dysphonia. It was adapted from Lee Silverman Voice Treatment (LSVT) and consists of four exercises: 1. Sustaining a loud /a/ for as long as possible, 2. Loud pitch glides up and down on /a/ over the entire range, 3. Using a loud and high voice for functional phrases specific to the participant, 4. Repeating those phrases in a loud and low voice.

PhoRTE and Vocal Function Exercises (VFE) have been shown to be quite helpful, and it is highly recommended that you work with a Speech Language Pathologist (SLP) to better understand what you are doing, learn to do them correctly, and be able to derive the full benefit from these exercises

This chapter can be disconcerting because of the many things that can go rogue with an aging voice. But with some attention and mindfulness on your part, there are many things that can be done to get back on pitch, smooth out a wobble, and keep your voice from crackling and popping. You don't have to have an old-sounding voice. You can restore and keep your beautiful, individual sound for speaking, singing, and having fun.

10

Vibrato and the older singer

Brenda Smith

Remember the day when your voice teacher or choral conductor said to you: "I am so pleased to hear a little vibrato in your voice!"? Maybe you were not completely certain whether to rejoice or retreat; but a small clue to the mystery of singing had been revealed. Your voice had gained a significant feature. Its presence made you "special" and perhaps even slightly more valued than you had been in its absence. Later in life, you learned that vibrato was considered a "vocal ornament" by the early vocal pedagogy authority, Ralph Appelman.[1] Your voice teacher may have explained that vibrato is the result of "all things being *right* in one's vocal technique" and you became proud of it. As life progressed, you discovered that a singer's vibrato rate may help her snatch an operatic role or might exclude her from a coveted position in a choral ensemble. As you gathered vocal colleagues, both amateur and professional, maybe you noted that some had an unevenness of vibrato, an erratic pulsation that annoyed you. Some of those voices may have presented with a rhythmic throbbing that resembled a squawk or a bleat. You heard an older voice that seemed completely out of control, his voice undulating over identifiable intervals when he sustained a single pitch. Did these experiences dim the glow of that unadulterated pride you once felt when your young, promising voice was imbued with an attractive shimmer? Perhaps you began to fear that you too might succumb to a case of vibrato rate frenzy. If so, here are three burning questions this article seeks to answer and explain:

- Question: Is a fitful vibrato the fate of the mature singer? Answer: No.

- Question: Are there strategies to rein in an unrestrained vibrato? Answer: Yes.

- Question: Is it ever too late to try? Answer: No.

Vibrato Rate

Vocal vibrato, its origin, and its measurement are popular research topics among voice scientists. With devices, researchers can calculate vibrato rate, diagram its shape, determine its symmetry and predict the impact of its asymmetry. The human ear, however, is the aesthetic authority over vibrato rate. Though voice teachers speak of symmetrical, controlled vibrato as a technical goal, scientific measurements have shown that some of most charismatic, exciting voices in the world present with wildly asymmetrical vibrato. The aesthetics of vibrato evolve from century to century. Regardless of scientific results, preferences regarding vibrato are utterly individual and idiosyncratic. In every era, when asked about vocal vibrato, most people say: "I know what I like". It is an answer spoken with conviction and often, without any explanation.

For those who teach voice, the presence of vibrato in a developing voice indicates a small technical milestone along the path to vocal maturity. The student, displaying a buoyant singer's posture, demonstrates a readiness that allows the power source of air to reach the vocal folds without inhibiting tensions. The vocal production is free and unencumbered. Such a clear, resonant voice is enlivened with an oscillating shimmer that enhances the tone quality and solidifies the tuning. This delicate balance between tone and breath support is guided by a mental attentiveness.

When you produced vibrato for the first time, were you aware that it was the result of good singing habits? Did anyone tell you that the vibrato emerged because your acquisition of vocal habits had aligned with a certain amount of physical ripening? Have you considered the specific elements that produce the valuable attribute known as "vibrato"? Hidden within this scenario are several applicable lessons for the older singer. Let's follow the steps that brought you as a young singer to this "moment of readiness".

Voice Training

It was the guidance of a teacher that steered you toward the "moment of readiness". The teacher modeled for you, monitoring your posture and breath efforts. How many of us continue to see a voice teacher regularly, once we are over 50 years of age? Vibrato rate changes incrementally as we age. Everyone needs a regular "check-up" with a qualified voice teacher or coach. Without good advice from an outside set of eyes and ears, every singer falls into habits that may bring unwanted consequences. Johan Sundberg noted that vibrato seems to develop "more or less by itself as voice training proceeds sucessfully."[2] At every age, a singing teacher or vocal coach can help you achieve and maintain an age and size appropriate vibrato. Even though you may think of it as inconvenient or unnecessary, voice training is a lifelong activity. Through regular voice study, you will develop the skills needed to manage vibrato rate during each season of life.

What if your vibrato rate is already a little out of control? Excessive vocal vibrato often presents in a singer who assumes that vibrato is inevitable and cannot be altered. The presence of unwanted motion in such a voice increases the stress level of the older singer, causing her to tighten her body. Self-consciousness grips more than just the mind. There is a visceral response that stops the air from flowing freely. The cycle of events is vicious. Suddenly, the singer is a victim of her own unhappy circumstances.

You can slow this cycle of unfortunate events. Consider the fact that your body and voice have been changing since you were born. You began life with a lighter, more transparent vocal quality. As you grew into adulthood, your body and voice increased in size. Your voice acquired an increased range, a distinct timbre, and a pleasing vibrato. As you matured, your vocal quality deepened in its hue. As physical changes within the larynx occur, your voice as an older singer is likely to have some additional motion. Your vocal quality changes because your vocal fold tissue and laryngeal cartilages change. You will discover that the process of ossification serves to stabilize the voice to some extent. These incremental changes are significant to note. When systematically addressed, you will be able to keep your voice in balance.

Your vibrato rate need not veer out of control. To avoid this situation, consult regularly with a trusted, knowledgeable professional, someone who could listen to your voice and give you constructive feedback. You need someone to monitor your singer's posture, your breath management and the health of your speaking voice. You are playing a musical instrument you can neither see nor touch. You may not require a weekly lesson nor will the content of the instruction be the same as it was in your youth. Everyone benefits from a frequent vocal "tune up" to obviate undesirable vocal habits.

Physical Fitness

When your instructor recognized vibrato in your voice the first time, you were probably a rather physically active and fit young person. The abdominal muscles upon which a singer depends for breath support need to remain supple and strong. Good physical conditioning is a contributing factor in the success of singers who continue to enjoy their voices over 50 years of age. Frankly, in the 21st century, it is difficult to provide a convincing argument for inactivity. Anyone can find a method for conditioning that will suit the constraints of location, physical limitations, and time. From yoga to Pilates, tai chi to qigong, kick boxing to water aerobics, our world is replete with possibilities for physical fitness. Every exercise regime has a version adapted to the older singer.

In our day, we speak of singers as "vocal athletes", people who use every aspect of their being to produce beautiful tone. To be fit as a singer, you must be physically active and able. Singing is not for the "couch potato". If you exercise carefully and frequently, you will have the physical attributes that will help you keep your voice and your vibrato rate in check. An exercise regimen keeps you mentally alert as well as physically robust. Singing, a mind-body activity, demands mental and physical conditioning to complement regular vocal exercise and training.

Mental attentiveness

Do you remember how surprised you were when your voice teacher first identified vibrato in your youthful tone? One reason you were unaware that your healthy vocalism produced a pleasing vibrato was because your mind was centered on the individual acts of singing. Because your teacher was in charge, you were not listening to your voice. You were "receiving" your voice. First, you imagined the pitch and vowel you hoped to sing. Then you guided the air with care and precision. You were living "in the moment", an instance of heightened anticipation. You awaited and obtained a beautiful vocal result.

As we age, our powers of concentration are compromised by myriad distractions. We are prone to sing "on automatic pilot". We sing to ourselves mindlessly when we drive, do chores or take walks. It is even possible to allow the mind to wander while singing familiar arias or choral parts. When this happens, we do not notice how we are producing tone or managing breath. Excessive vibrato may result when a singer sinks unknowingly into such unhealthy vocal habits.

To sing well, we must remain mindful. Healthy singing requires extreme concentration on a multitude of tasks such as pitch, vowel, and breath management. With rapt attention, we must address the exquisite steps required to produce a healthy singing tone. It is not uncommon for an older singer to drift into the habit of singing down the octave or to allow the speaking voice to drone in a monotone. In choral ensembles, older women join tenor sections while older men begin to cultivate the lowest octave of the keyboard. These behaviors interrupt the innate maturation process and disguise the original character of a voice. The natural vibrato will be obscured, too. As you age, discipline yourself to use your voice judicially and respectfully. Allow your speaking voice to lilt and your singing voice to soar.

Vocal exercise

How to regain lost vocal control, you ask? You already have a powerful tool in your toolbox that will help you. It is the trusted, time-honored *bel canto* exercise called *messa di voce* ("measuring the voice"). It may be the very exercise your voice teacher used to help you find your vibrato in the first place. Start with the following exercise model to regain your strength, coordination and vocal control:

1. Begin to include the gentle crescendo and decrescendo of a single pitch in your daily regimen. Choose a pitch that lies in a comfortable middle range. While mimicking the act of chewing, begin to hum the pitch. Allow it to increase in loudness and to decrease very symmetrically. By using a chewing motion, you will avoid unwanted jaw and tongue tension.

2. Next, using a carefully balanced onset of sound, phonate your favorite vowel. Concentrate on the pitch and vowel as you steadily release breath pressure and crescendo. Strive to decrease the volume as consistently as you increased it. Stop before you feel any tension. Relax and repeat.

As you "measure" your voice, you enhance your physical coordination and strength. These improvements will help you stabilize your vibrato and reestablish control of your voice.

Because the cartilages of the larynx ossify during aging, you may find agile musical passages to be more challenging. Include agility exercises in your daily warm up regimen to help you maintain flexibility in your singing. The practice of agile passages has proven a deterrent to excessive vibrato. Try this exercise model to develop control over vibrato:

1. Choose a comfortable pitch in middle range. Sing a descending five tone pattern on a nonsense syllable such as "doo" [du] and perform a *messa di voce* on the vowel "oo" [u] during the final note. Pace the *messa di voce* by reiterating the vowel [u] in your mind to achieve a crescendo over four counts and decrescendo over four counts. Literally, "measure" your singing with your mind, voice and breath. Relax, breathe and repeat in transposition.

2. Now, advance the exercise by removing the consonant. Sing the entire pattern on the vowel "oo" [u] being very careful to achieve a balanced onset of sound.

3. Next, sing an ascending and descending pattern with an extended, consistent *messa di voce* on the vowel of the final note.

As your skill level increases, design advanced exercises based upon this model.

Gentle, balanced onset

Notice the admonitions regarding a gentle, balanced onset of sound? It is another hallmark of *bel canto* singing. Younger singers are known to be a bit impatient, often using the glottal plosive to start the tone. Older singers can be lethargic in their engagement of the breath management muscles. A balanced vocal onset requires the perfect timing of buoyant breath with pitch and vowel.

To recover your ability to coordinate air with tone, select a favorite lullaby. Cradle an imaginary beloved child or pet in your arms and sing with a soothing vocal tone. Notice how gently you breathe to prepare for the singing. Observe how sweetly and effortlessly you begin to sing. You have rediscovered the timing and skill inherent in producing a gentle onset. Frequent glottal interventions in the onset of vocal sound can be an underlying cause for unwanted, unpleasant vibrato. The character of your breathing determines much about the character of the sound produced by it. By retrieving your ability to achieve this coordinated onset or "flow phonation", you strike a perfect balance between breath pressure and vocal fold activation. This skill forms the cornerstone of a steady vibrato.

Repertoire

How we sing matters and what we sing matters, too. Effective voice teachers would say they "agonize" over repertoire assignments, seeking to find works that fit not just the voice, but also the personality of an emerging singer. The choices your voice teacher made for you as a young singer were crucial to your vocal growth. They helped determine the success of your singing career. As you aged, you began to make repertoire decisions for yourself. You may have chosen repertoire that you had always wanted to sing. Did you consider carefully the implications of your choices? Did you seek advice about how the repertoire might impact your vocal life? If not, the repertoire may not have fit your vocal capacities. You may have pressed your voice into service and created the circumstances that produce excess vibrato.

Each of us must consider the performing forces and the emotional expectations of any repertoire. Some voices perform easily over symphony orchestras, but many do not. There are times in our lives when singing with a harpsichord, lute or piano is indicated. At other times, some of us will have the good fortune of singing with a chamber ensemble or orchestra. There are times when amplification can be used to help us avoid vocal strain. If we seek repertoire and performing circumstances that are appropriate to our age, size and abilities, we can preserve our natural vocal gifts and minimize the pressed phonation often associated with excessive vibrato. Let the incremental changes associated with aging inform your approach to repertoire.

At the peak of a career, when the voice is plush and pliable, a performer can fulfill completely the composer's intentions. Such a consummate performance is the goal of every singer. In later years, vocal forces diminish. If you recognize these limitations and redirect your energies toward more achievable goals, you will lengthen your singing life. Renée Fleming's recent retirement of the role of the *Marschallin* in Richard Strauss' *Der Rosenkavalier* sets a precedent for the wise, well-timed shaping of an outstanding vocal career. Ms. Fleming's prudent choice, after more than 70 performances of the coveted role, has sealed her vocal gift in the minds and hearts of her admirers. She has likely extended her professional career and preserved her vocal resources. Her example teaches us that we should not remain committed to repertoire that felt comfortable once, but is no longer vocally suitable.

Once you had achieved vibrato and developed stability as a young singer, your teacher began to assign repertoire that plumbed deeper levels of pathos. You advanced from ballad-like songs on texts in the third person to operatic arias in the first person. Instead of singing about the experience of someone else, you were required to "embody" a role, generally that of a character who was entangled in complicated emotional struggles. You learned to express feeling through melodic material that was enriched harmonically to depict deep emotion. As you met such assignments, your growing voice attained a greater presence of sound and substance. You sang vocal works that demanded greater accompanying forces. The piano accompanist fully lifted the lid to produce more support for your growing vocal tone. Because of your vocal maturity, you may have been given opportunities to sing chamber works or orchestral settings of songs and arias. Through this process, your vibrato rate became more established and defined. Your vibrato became the "vocal ornament" that Appleman described.

As an older singer, you will want to reverse the process. Remember: Vibrato rate is not just a physical issue; it is also an emotional one. An older singer who wishes to sing with less vibrato should search for repertoire that approaches passions and pathos with restraint. Look for musical settings that invite a cooler, less complex tone quality. Sing works that require reduced accompanying forces. Be sensible about the key of the selection. Avoid keys that exploit uncomfortable transitions in your vocal range.

Why not branch out and learn vocal repertoire that demands clearer tonal textures? If you choose wisely, you may have more opportunities to participate longer in the public sphere. Try learning a few of the *Frühe Lieder* of Arnold Schoenberg instead of performing your favorites from Robert Schumann's *Frauenliebe und-Leben*. Substitute a Reynaldo Hahn *mélodie* for the cherished "Vocalise" of Sergei Rachmaninoff.

Sing a Schubert Lied instead of a Wagnerian aria, a song by Ivor Gurney instead of the "Some Enchanted Evening" from Rodgers & Hammerstein's *South Pacific*. The investigation of unfamiliar repertoire will invigorate your mind and musical senses, while helping you adapt your voice and technique. You will begin to educate your listener about music of value that is rarely performed. In the process, you are creating for yourself a performance setting that is free of the expectations associated with works from the familiar repertory. Relax and enjoy a fresh chapter in your singing life!

Listening

During your student years, your voice teacher guided your pursuit of a personal sound ideal. Your listening list included aural examples of professional singers whose voices would be good models for you in the future. Evaluate your current listening list. Do the voices that please you bear similarities with your own voice at this point in your development? Are you clinging to models that do not reflect the inevitable physical changes you are experiencing? Most singers feel very loyal to specific singers and interpretations. Perhaps your favorite models are no longer appropriate examples.

A reduction in vocal range, agility, and stamina occurs as your voice ages. As mentioned above, because of the thinning of vocal fold tissue and the reduction of lubrication and flexibility, your voice may become lighter and more lyric. How does an older singer imitate a younger sound? Vocal, tonal memory is a part of the vocal gift. In seeking a clearer, more translucent sound ideal for yourself, you might want to limit your exposure temporarily to less dramatic, leaner voices. By listening to valid vocal models that exhibit delicate tone colors, you may facilitate the metamorphosis of your vocal identity. Through listening, you will develop an appreciation for a younger generation of singers and an acquaintance with exciting, new interpretations. These insights will be valuable to your growth as a musician and performer.

The secret to graceful vocal aging can be found in the anticipation of inevitable changes and the implementation of useful strategies that combat them. Consider the reality of comparable circumstances in the other fields. In the acting world, young actresses play the role of the ingénue for a measured time, before assuming more mature acting roles. In sports, elite players retire to become trainers and coaches. The aging singer need not leave the stage or abandon the playing field. Singers can sing for a lifetime if they modify the vocal expectations while maintaining consistent physical conditioning.

Sound ideal

What about the sound of your voice? How can you achieve a simpler, more youthful sound? During your early training, you learned that every tone you phonate must first be "audiated" mentally. You imagined the pitch and vowel in your mind before you produced it. Your teacher may have asked you to use a hand gesture to help you coordinate your thinking with your singing. Try to gauge your audiation toward a daintier, straighter sound. As you prepare to phonate, think of yourself as a much younger singer. You may wish to imagine yourself to be a dozen years younger or you may prefer to imitate the voice of a younger performer you admire. Peel away those layers of color and pathos and you will produce a vocal quality that is more versatile and malleable. That is not how I should sound, you say? Ask your teacher, coach, or best friend and you may be surprised at the response.

With each decade, the fundamental frequency of the voice adjusts subtly in pitch. When older singers sense that the fundamental pitch is lower, they frequently react by applying pressure to the sound, darkening and thickening their voices. Older singers face life style changes that may isolate them from others. Some may suffer from hearing loss. It becomes easy for older singers to decrease their daily voice use. When they do sing, they may sing more to themselves than to others. Any of these circumstances can have an impact on vibrato rate. To avoid these phenomena, lighten and brighten your sound ideal and toss the tone toward a distant target. The mental, vocal and physical effort of these strategies gives the voice direction. In the process, the vibrato will be less troublesome and more pleasing.

Sensations of resonance

In your basic voice training, you were admonished to memorize the sensations of resonance rather than trusting your ears. You learned to feel the sensations of resonance and to delight in them. This concept is especially important to you as an older singer. Once you have begun to sing, do not listen to your sound. Keep your mind on the pitch, the vowel, the rhythm and the meaning of the text. Continue to feed breath to your tone.

It is very difficult to accept the fact that your ear cannot hear your own voice as others do. At any age, the singer's ears should not be the principal monitor for the quality of vocal tone. Our ears deceive us by providing only partial feedback. In any other situation, you would not make changes based on limited information. Singing requires a substantial amount of risk taking. Before phonation, a singer sends neurological signals for pitch and vowel as breath is engaged. The resulting vocal result is a revelation, heard fully by the listeners only. Through trial and error, a singer learns to rely upon the positive sensations of resonance and "ring" that have been coaxed into being by a teacher or coach. Regular lessons and daily practice keep the kinesthetic sensations familiar and fresh.

An older singer may be skeptical, believing that hearing one's own voice is possible and productive. This belief will cause the singer to apply unnecessary muscle tension to the throat and body during singing. It is likely that excessive vibrato will be the result. Stop trying to monitor your own voice with your ear. Learn to trust the reliable sensations of resonance. The sensations free your voice and minimize its motion.

Choral singing

Singing should always be an inclusive activity. Most singers wish to sing with others. Is there an expiration date for choral singing, you may ask? The choral art allows for every voice to participate at any age. For an older singer, a fear that his vibrato rate might deter him from a favorite choral group can be very real. In certain choral organizations, like the Mormon Tabernacle Choir, age or years of service may limit a singer's involvement. If the ensemble specializes in *a cappella* music of the Medieval period, the older singer may feel unpleasantly confined by the restraints the repertoire itself poses on his singing. In most other settings, a singer can remain a treasured member of the ensemble by following a few simple principles.

Discipline yourself

Maintain your commitment to good vocal hygiene and the basics of singing (Relaxation, Posture, Breathing, and Resonance). Stretch your body and warm up your voice before attending the rehearsal. As a chorister, assume a buoyant singer's posture. When seated in the rehearsal, sit erect in your seat. It may be necessary for you to equip yourself with a pillow for back support or a box upon which to rest your feet. Carry as little music in your choral folder as possible, so that its weight will not strain your arms and shoulders. Bring a source for hydration.

Share only your best ingredients

Take frequent breaks during the rehearsal. Choral music is the blending of many voices into a single, corporate tone. The concept of choral breathing allows each singer to depart and return from the corporate choral tone. Each chorister brings a certain complement of vocal ingredients to be shared. Choirs work best if each member learns to share only the best ones. As a younger singer, your ability to sustain a pitch may have been one of your finest contributions. As an older singer, you may wish to take a breath during a long note value and enter again a little later. At times, you may prefer "to listen more than you sing".[3] For example, when your choral section presents the melismatic fugue subject in a choral work, refrain from singing. Listen attentively as your section colleagues deliver it. Begin to sing at the point in the work when the musical texture thickens.

Remember: Choral singing has a different goal than solo singing. Be sure that you "turn the knob" from solo singing technique to a healthy choral one, a tone that invites the harmonic properties of other voice parts. This can be done by elongating the jaw and rounding the lips. Strive for a relaxed breath and a welcoming, flexible vocal sound. Breathe when necessary and appreciate the role you play in the ensemble. If you bring your best skills to the project, you will continue to be an asset to the endeavor for years to come.

Relax and enjoy

When surrounded by young voices that are vibrant and virile, an older singer might experience negative feelings such as intimidation, sadness or even anger. Stop for a moment and consider the situation from the viewpoint of the younger colleagues. Put yourself in their shoes. They are striving to establish their vocal habits. Some are reaching their peak performance levels. At the same time, they may be very concerned about their futures. Your presence as a senior statesperson in the choir proves to them that better days will lie ahead. In their current lives, they rise regularly to challenges and collapse occasionally in defeat. Drama may be their daily bread. You have a lifetime of accomplishments upon which you can lean. Your life is probably more predictable and less explosive. Your role in the choir has changed, but it is of equal value. Surrender your ego and let the younger ones assume responsibility for the exposed passages in the music. Relax and remember how well you achieved such vocal feats earlier in life. By doing so, you will breathe more fully and calmly. Your voice will be more in your control. You will be able to enjoy the benefits that singing with others affords for as long as you like.

Real life stories

"Lo, how a Rose e'er blooming"[4]

In 1996, I stepped in front of a choir of senior citizens for the first time. Having worked with community choruses, church choirs and professional ensembles for decades, I felt relatively well-prepared to help singers over 50. The challenge proved greater than I had anticipated, partly because there was little to no scientific or pedagogical literature on the topic, at that time. After only a few sessions, an 80-year old alto, representing her peers, asked: "Why does my voice shake?" Her honest question surprised me, and it certainly deserved a straightforward answer. I asked her if she knew what vibrato was, where it came from, and how it can be maintained. As we deconstructed the individual elements, the mystery unraveled. We concluded the rehearsal with an experiment. It was a series of steps that brought the choir to the kind of "moment of readiness" described at the outset of this article.

Step I: Exercises to relax muscle tension in the body and release anxiety

Step II: Establishment of a good seated posture.

Step III: Exhalation exercises to expel unwanted air

Step IV: Inhalation exercises to receive breath energy

Step V: Easy descending sigh patterns connecting air to vocal tone

Step VI: *Messa di voce* exercises on a single, medium pitch on the vowel "oo" [u].

Next, I asked the singers to imagine themselves to be Vienna Choir Boys in St. Stephen's Cathedral on Christmas Eve and invited them to sing "Lo, how a Rose e'er blooming" on the vowel "oo" [u]. Each singer used hand motions to guide the sound forward to a distant, imaginary altar. The result was a pleasingly unified choral tone that displayed even, unobtrusive vibrato.

What produced this appealing result? It was the result of everything being "right". Relaxation, posture, breathing and resonance had been established. The singers imagined a youthful sound ideal and concentrated very carefully on the pitch, the vowel and the direction of the breath. They did not listen to their own voices. They sent their voices to a specific point, using a gesture that guided the breath and kept the body relaxed and free. The steps built a foundation for further effective voice building and vibrato management. Use these steps to achieve equally positive outcomes for yourself.

"A Rose touched by the Sun's Warm Rays"[5]

Since 2004, I have worked with a group of 60 singers who reside in a continuing care retirement community in Florida. The singers range in age from 65 to 95 years. One of the most notable of the singers is a 92-year old soprano, who has logged 72 years of vocal training. She is an amateur singer, the identical twin of a professional singer. She combines her devotion to the art of singing with a rigorous physical conditioning program. She believes that her study of vocal repertoire has kept her mentally alert and spiritually invigorated. She has negotiated a fluid transition throughout decades of singing, monitoring the tiniest of physical and vocal changes. In times of grief or stress, she has lowered her vocal and performance expectations. In better times, she has challenged herself to meet higher goals. To maintain a beautiful vocal quality, she retools her technique from day to day. She continues to sing lyrically. Her voice is light, agile, and embellished with an appropriate, shimmering vibrato. She performs publicly to an appreciative audience and provides the promise of lifelong singing to everyone who hears her.

Let these examples from real life situations serve as models as you strive to develop greater vocal control. Evaluate critically your skills and habits. Vibrato is the result of many elements coexisting in perfect balance. Are any basic elements slightly out of balance or even, missing? Is your sound ideal age and size appropriate? In the act of singing, do you remain utterly alert to the "order of things"? To maintain this equilibrium, revisit each element (relaxation, posture, breath, and resonance) regularly. Practice regularly. Keep active and "in the singing game".

Final thoughts

Vocal vibrato appears when physical and spiritual maturity meet vocal technique and mental readiness. Vibrato becomes an identifying feature in a voice, but it should not become a detriment. If the singer continues to hone technical skills, the voice and its vibrato will mature incrementally. It is hoped that you will "make friends" with your vibrato. Its rate changes with your state of being. If you are nervous or agitated, the vibrato rate may increase. If you are tired or listless, the vibrato may be lugubrious. Good vocal and physical fitness aid in keeping the means and extremes in check.

There comes a moment in the life of an astute person when certain vocal goals are no longer reasonable. Following an honest assessment by qualified professionals, the aging singer can embark on a course of discovery to find different yet satisfying outlets for further vocal growth. No one can reverse the aging of a voice. Each of us must learn to accept voice changes and adjust to them. The singing skills learned in youth must be trained, strengthened and retooled regularly.

Voice changes occur to varying degrees throughout a singing life. Throughout life, the vocal transition begun during puberty needs to be nurtured every day. Each of us as a youngster had a "cambiata" or changing voice. Our teachers admonished us to sing only the notes that were available and comfortable. Sometimes, our teachers rewrote a passage of the music to fit our specific skill level. The principle applies throughout life. An adult singer may lack access to specific notes or ranges from time to time.

Medications, physical ailments, stressful events or emotional changes might alter vocal quality and destabilize vibrato. The changes themselves need not trouble you. Seek help and acquire useful coping strategies. Be proactive when vocal deficits appear. Do not ignore subtle differences. When accepting a diagnosis or prescription, ask the physician about possible contraindications that might compromise the voice. Find an experienced, qualified vocal pedagogue with whom you feel comfortable. Share honestly the history of your singing life and your concerns about your voice's current tendencies. Keep the doors of communication open between you, your voice and the trusted professional whose objective assessment can help you sustain your skills. No one anticipates every change that might occur, but good information and advice are readily available if you seek it.

References and Notes

1. Appelman R, (1967). *The Science of Vocal Pedagogy.* Bloomington: Indiana University Press; 23.
2. Sundberg J, (1987), *The Science of the Singing Voice.* DeKalb: Northern Illinois University Press; 163.
3. Helen Kemp (1918-2015) was one of America's foremost experts on choral singing and children. Dr. Kemp is best known for her motto: "Body, mind, spirit, voice – it takes a whole person to sing and rejoice." She herself was a lifelong singer and educator. In her workshops, she often featured a poster with the phrase: "Listen more than you sing."
4. "Lo, how a Rose e'er blooming" is the English translation of the German hymn "Es ist ein Ros entsprungen". The original text was written anonymously in Cologne, Germany in 1599 and set to music by Michael Praetorius (1571-1621).
5. "A Rose touched by the Sun's warm rays" is a Pennsylvania Dutch hymn text by Maria Brubacher, translated and set to music by Jean Berger (1909-2002). The choral setting was published in Minneapolis, MN by Augsburg Fortress in 1962.

Further reading

Books

Callaghan J. (2014) *Singing & Science: Body, Brain & Voice* Oxford: Compton Publishing.
Heman-Ackah, Y.D., Sataloff R.T., Hawkshaw M. (2013) *The Voice: A Medical Guide for Achieving and Maintaining a Healthy Voice* Narberth, PA: Science and Medicine.
Malde M, Allen K, Zeller MJ. (2009) *What Every Singer Needs to Know About the Body*, San Diego, CA: Plural Publishing.
Meredith V. (2007) *Sing Better as You Age: A Comprehensive Guide for Adult Choral Singer*, Santa Barbara, CA: Santa Barbara Music Publishing.
Miller R. (1996) *The Structure of Singing*. New York: Schirmer.
Olson M. (2010) *The Solo Singer in the Choral Setting: A Handbook for Achieving Vocal Health* Lanham, MD: Scarecrow Press.
Seashore CE, ed. (1932) *The Vibrato: University of Iowa Studies in the Psychology of Music*, 1932; Vol. I. Iowa City, IA: University of Iowa.
Smith, B. (2005) *Cantare et Sonare: A Handbook of Choral Performance Practice*. Chapel Hill, NC: Hinshaw Music.
Smith B., Sataloff R.T. (2013) *Choral Pedagogy*, 3ed. San Diego, CA: Plural Publishing; 2013.
Smith B., Sataloff R.T. (2013) *Choral Pedagogy and the Older Singer*. San Diego, CA: Plural Publishing.
Sundberg J. (1987) *The Science of the Singing Voice*. DeKalb, IL: Northern Illinois University Press.

Book chapters and journal articles

Anand S., Wingate J., Smith B. and Shrivastav R. (2012) Acoustic Parameters Critical for an Appropriate Vibrato *Journal of Voice* 26(6): 819–25.
Gabrielsson A., Juslin P.N. (1996) Emotional expression in music performance between the performer's intentions and the listener's experience *Psychology of Music* 24: 68–91.
Sataloff R.T., Linville S.E. (2006) The Effects of Age on the Voice in *Vocal Health and Pedagogy: Advanced Assessment and Treatment* 2ed., Vol II San Diego, CA: Plural Publishing, pp 17–31.
Smith B. (2007) Speaking and Singing in One Voice *The Church Music Quarterly*, Royal College of Church Music, March.
Smith B. (1996) Voice Building for Choirs *The American Organist* Spring.
Smith B., Sataloff R.T (2013) Singing for a Lifetime: Perpetuating Intergenerational Choirs *Choral Journal: Community Choir Focus Issue* 53(May) 16–25.
Strempel E.L. (2006) The Shifting Aesthetics of Vibrato *Journal of Singing* 62: 405–411.
Sundberg J. (1999) The Perception of Singing in *The Psychology of Music*, 2ed. San Diego, CA: Academic Press, pp 171–214.

11

New normals

Sharon L. Radionoff

As we travel the road of life, there are many twists, turns and experiences that write the chapters of our lives. During these chapters there are a multitude of events: 1) school milestones, 2) career building, 3) career changes, 4) family growth, 5) retirement and 6) there may also be many health challenges that mark our paths. Anything we experience through life has the potential to affect the voice. We are a whole person comprised of body, mind and spirit. Some of the things which we experience happen directly to us – i.e. physical issues. Other issues affect us indirectly such as a death of a loved one. Therefore physical, psychological and spiritual issues may all have a bearing on one's overall health therefore, vocal health. We often take our health and our voice for granted. As some say 'we don't know what we have until we lose it.'

While we recognize that the aging voice is not the only group who experiences life/voice changes or 'new normals', this chapter focuses on this demographic.

When younger and in school, the main focus of life is school and what we are training for. Once the career starts, and family begins to change, the focus is divided among more variables. The pie does not get bigger it is only cut into more pieces! It really is not fair to compare then and now. There seems to be a tendency within all of us to compare "I remember when..." with our current status, often putting our past memories on a pedestal.

When we experience vocal difficulty, in order to move forward vocally and psychologically it is necessary to 'embrace the now.' As humans, we are on a continual journey of change. At the Sound Singing Institute, we are never sure when starting the journey together where it will take us... I encourage all to be willing the embrace the potential new normal.

As stated earlier, voice changes can happen as result of direct causes such as vocal fold surgeries. Other surgeries and illnesses also have the potential to change the voice, because the body is the voice. It is normal when experiencing difficulty to try to fix what we don't like. Sometimes this is on a conscious level, while sometimes it is subconscious, and we can easily get into a habit of manipulating to try to 'fix.' I refer to this as 'making' not 'allowing'. In essence, it is the opposite of efficiency. When the body allows for efficiency, it is all about allowing not making. Therefore, the job of the singing voice specialist is to help the patient find balance again so that the body will once again work for them! Secondly, training may lead back to a balance or alignment which seems familiar or it may be a 'new normal' in pitch center (higher or lower), total range, flexibility, stamina, power and so on.

If indeed there is a new normal, it will take time for all of the muscles needed to get used to their new jobs. Along with vocal fold surgeries, life challenges that can precipitate the need for rebalancing include other surgeries, memory issues, hearing loss, death of family and friends, and moving from a lifelong home.

Below are 5 case studies which describe a variety of medical and function issues. Each case will highlight pertinent beneficial exercises. Please refer to the Recommended exercises section at the end of this chapter for a more thorough discourse of exercises used for each case.

Case 1: 51-year-old female

KS is a 51-year-old female who holds a degree in accounting. She is a CPA and business manager by day and sings in a choir for enjoyment and love. During her initial evaluation at the Sound Singing Institute, she stated that she has always sung as well as accompany choirs. She stated that she used to play guitar and sing in the summers. After college she joined a Catholic church choir where she was introduced to classical music. She sang for many weddings and enjoyed cantoring often. She did not formally take voice lessons until many years later. She stated that she sang for a friend's 20th Anniversary and a week later she cantored at mass. Not long after that she stated that she became ill with bronchitis and pneumonia. She stated that the voice started coming back a bit but that she had another bout of bronchitis not long after.

KS stated that she finally saw an otolaryngologist specializing in voice. Under the procedure of strobovideolaryngoscopy she was diagnosed with incomplete closure of the vocal folds, reflux, muscle tension dysphonia and tremor in the right vocal fold. She stated that she worked with a speech pathologist but that it did not help her singing voice.

During her initial singing evaluation KS exhibited vocal tremor, jaw, neck and tongue tension. Along with this was an arched lower back and body weight too far forward.

Exercises recommended

(non-IPA used throughout this chapter)

1. Duh jaw
2. Single repeated notes on /soo-soo-soop/ and /boo-boo-boop/
3. Small step-wise patterns
   a. 1-7-1, 1-2-1
   b. using /boo-boo-boop/

Update: KS reported that her voice was better and that she thought often about letting her jaw hang thinking duh.

Additional exercises

1. Airflow using /huh/, /wh/, /sh/, /s/, /f/,
   a. Back, side, sitting with air keyboard
2. more sounds were used for small patterns: /boo-woo-woo/, and /soo-woo-woop/

We began to realize that when dealing with her tremor if we were able to use a different rate of repetition of sound then the rhythm of the tremor, that the sound became more 'normal' sounding to her (using /boom/ and /weem/)

(see the example page – numbers refer to scale degrees)

Example:

♩ ♩ ♫ ♫ ♩
3- 2- 1- 1- 1- 1- 1

♩ ♩ ♩ ♩ ♫ ♫ ♩
1- 2- 3- 2- 1- 1-1-1- 1

Also, a series was helpful using /doom/

♪♪♪♪♪♪♪♪ ♩
3-3-2-2-1-1-1-1- 1

♩ ♩ ♪♪ ♩
3- 2- 1- 1- 1

♩ ♩ ♩
3- 2- 1

♪♪ ♪♪
3-1- 3-1

She was further successful in transferring this to chanting small song phrases using

/doom/ + 'p' for offset

Update: KS stated that her family has been traveling a lot for her youngest son in baseball. She stated that this actually helps, because she is able to try transferring this idea into songs at another church. Since they don't know her and will probably never be seen there again, it gives her more freedom and permission to try.

Additional exercises

1. Chant scripture reading and poems along with songs on a comfortable pitch starting on /doom/

2. Descendings: Legato – starting somewhere comfortable and coming down using: /foo/, /floo/, /floom/, /floam/, /flihm/, /fleem/, /fweem/, /fwahm-wahm/, /flahm-lahm/, /fwaem/, /daem/, /dihm/, /deem/, /doom/, and /dohm/

    KS stated that it seems to help her to think chanting. Further, the idea of legato and the rhythmic repetition, upon clinical observation, helps KS to circumvent the tremor.

3. Rhythmic repetition sequence

    ♪♪♪♪♩ ♩♩♩ ♩♩♩
    a. 3-3-2-2-1,   3- 2- 1,   3 2- 1

    b. Using /wee-wee-weep/

4. Exercise to transfer the legato/chant production to skipping pattern 3-1 /weem-p/

Update: KS stated at her next session that she feels like her voice is more stable whether she is sitting at the keyboard accompanying and singing or in the choir loft singing.

Additional exercises

1. Woo Circles were introduced next.

2. Quick consonant and vowel shifting on single notes and descendings.

Update: At her next session KS stated that even though her home stress level was very high due to health difficulties of their oldest son, she is able to keep the stability of the efficient use of breath and legato when singing at church.

Case 2: 57-year-old male

HV is a 57-year-old male professional singer who has sung leading rolls at the Metropolitan Opera, San Francisco, Los Angeles, San Diego, Cleveland, and Orlando opera companies along with soloist appearances with many Symphony Orchestras. He is also considered a master teacher and adjudicator of national and international competitions. He began to experience vocal difficulty and saw an otolaryngologist specializing in voice and underwent the procedure of strobovideolaryngoscopy. The patient complained of the onset starting two weeks ago of an acute singing problem that was moderately severe. He stated that he was experiencing trouble breathing. Other symptoms included a cough and post-nasal drainage. He stated that when he sang in Arizona that the singing didn't feel right but that it didn't feel like a cold. He further stated that he has to work harder, has no head voice or access to falsetto. He is concerned because he has a concert that will be coming up soon. Under examination it appears that the peri-arytenoid tissue is edematous and hyperemic, and the sub-glottic tissue was also edematous and hyperemic in appearance. He was diagnosed with GERD and put on a PPI.

History at the SSI

HV did not feel that the PPI was improving the situation sufficiently, so he came to the Sound Singing Institute for an evaluation and session. He stated that he has the following medical conditions: Asthma, allergies, swallowing problems, ADD, neck pain, hiatal hernia, diverticulitis and possibly migraines.

HV is proactive toward staying in good health. He exercises (walk, bike, swim), he eats a healthy diet (watches carbohydrate intake) and sleeps well.

He stated that he had a contract in NY one year ago and was very ill for 3 weeks. He stated that a month ago he had an audition coming up and was working on new songs but that he felt like he was working too hard and that his voice felt heavy. He further stated that he wakes up and phonation is clean but it becomes more difficult as the day goes on.

During the singing evaluation he exhibited tongue, neck and ribcage tension along with excessive glottal pressure during phonation.

Exercises recommended

1. Lizard tongue – using bleh with sound
2. Airflow using /s/, /sh/, and /f/
    a. standing
    b. with moving arms and torso
3. Single note stepwise patterns
    a. 1-2-1, 1-7-1, 1-7-1-2-1, 1-2-1-7-1
    b. Using /boom/, /bloom/, /floom-loom/
4. Pairs on B2, C3
    a. using /s-z-s/, /f-v-f/, /sh-zh-sh/, /th-th-th/
5. Highly recommended seeing a chiropractor
6. Highly recommended getting a massage with focus of neck and shoulders
7. He will see a GI doc and have an endoscopy done
8. He will begin allergy shots
9. He has been asked to be aware of pressure and tightening in his speaking voice since this has the potential to affect the singing voice agility

Update: HV reported that he is having much success with chiropractics and massage. He stated that his head voice access is definitely better.

Additional exercises

1. Slides
   a. Using unvoiced/voiced pairs
   b. Descending, wavy and rollercoaster

2. Discussed the acid watcher diet by Jonathan Aviv

Update: HV reported noticing more flexibility in his singing voice and less pressure when speaking. He stated that he feels better because he is losing a little bit of weight.

Additional exercises

3. Falsetto rollercoaster /foh-woo/, /foh-wee/

Update: HV reported feeling more relief in the neck and that the tension is releasing. He further stated that things are beginning to improve, and he is able to warm up higher. He also stated that he has been exercising a lot (walking and biking) and that his reflux has subsided. HV is almost at the maintenance level with allergy shots. He stated that his overall tightness is resolving and that he feels looser overall. He reported that he now has 'fluency' on the top and is able to vocally demonstrate again. HV stated that he feels more confident, and ready for his concert.

Update: HV performed his concert in New Mexico. He stated that although his voice became dry at intermission, overall the voice behaved very well. He reported that he had a bit of post-concert body tightness and saw the chiropractor for maintenance. HV stated that he no longer feels vocally limited.

Case 3: 57-year-old female

PP is a 57-year-old female who is a contemporary church service choir and solo singer. PP was a Music major at Sam Houston State University when sustained multiple injuries in a serious car accident. Her jaw was broken, ankle crushed, her leg was broken in 3 places and she had a closed head injury. Furthermore, she was 'trached' post-accident. Apparently, she was seen by an ENT at the time who stated that she only had a hairline vocal fold opening. PP was in a coma for 2 months.

PP stated that she had outpatient therapy for 9 months to a year and that memory was very difficult. She was told that she has sustained damage to the brain stem. Post physical therapy, she stated that her voice seemed relatively ok, but that she had a much shorter range. Recently she saw an otolaryngologist specializing in voice because she stated that she was experiencing extreme shortness of breath and that her range is now only that of the interval of a 5th. Under strobovideolaryngoscopy, she was diagnosed with right vocal fold paresis and vocal fatigue along with Muscle Tension Dysphonia (MTD). She was referred to the Sound Singing Institute to see if it would be possible to gain better closure and eradicate her medial/lateral MTD. If not, then possible vocal fold augmentation would be discussed.

During her initial singing evaluation PP exhibited shallow abdominal/diaphragmatic breathing, head/neck elevation and protrusion, tongue retraction, jaw tension, and neck tension.

It was apparent during the first session with the singing voice specialist, that brain processing was slow and that things had to be repeated often.

Exercises recommended

1. Airflow using /wh/, /sh/, /s/, /f/
   a. sitting
   b. repeat each sound 5 x's in a row

There was a careful, slow, long discussion at the patients request to understand how each airflow sound was made. This included lip shape, tongue shape, placement of tongue, tongue tip and teeth on lip for the /f/.

2. Single note repeated on B3 and C4
   a. using /boom/, /bloom/

There was another discussion in regard to taking away an unhealthy controller (her neck muscles creating MTD) and exchanging it with a healthy controller i.e. the use of the lips for the plosive /b/ and the nasalant /m/. We also discussed the creation of a feedback loop using legato /boom-boom-boom/ or /bloom-bloom-bloom/ repetitions.

3. small step-wise patterns
   a. 1-7-1, 1-2-1
   b. using /boom-boom-boom/

We discussed the benefit of using a checklist when practicing.

1. jaw relaxed (home alone face – hands on face – or thinking 'duh')

2. pouty pucker (not tight)

3. tongue tip (behind bottom front teeth for /b/, /m/ and the vowel /oo/)

Update: At the next session PP stated that she feels that she has body challenges with weight and wonders if she may have thyroid issues. She said that is seems like her body energy stays very low constantly.

We discussed the concept of 'permission to play' since so many chores seem difficult – I encouraged her to get out her grandchildren's crayons and a coloring book and to use them for herself.

Additional exercises

1. pairs /s-z-s/ on B3 and G3

2. increased sounds used with single note repeated
   a. /bleem/, /beem/, /blihm/

Update: At her next session, PP stated that her biggest frustration was her personal time management. We discussed strategies for helping her to get in her 'games' for voice. We added more pairs sounds (/f-v-f/, /sh-zh-sh/) as well as longer patterns (1-2-1-7-1, 1-7-1-2-1, 1-2-3-2-1, 1-2-3-4-3-2-1). I have also encouraged her to continue with coloring and/or painting. She also stated that she went to choir practice since I saw her last. She stated that she had a very difficult time. We discussed the concept of 'staying in your own lane' and not comparing yourself and current abilities to other people.

Additional exercises

1. Introduced many new sounds to repeated singles
   A. /soom/, /shoom/, /foom/, /floom/, /floom – loom/

2. worked on the unvoiced and voiced /th/ sounds. These are very difficult for her.

3. Have begun chanting song texts on B3 starting with the set-up /floom/

Update: At her next session PP stated that she will be a counselor at a church camp for 1 month. She stated that they have already secured a golf cart to be able to get around the property easier. She also stated that she wants to prepare to sing a song at the women's retreat in 1 month but must find a song with a very small range.

Additional exercises

1. continue to increase the sounds used in repeated singles
   a. /seem/, /sheem/, /feem/, /fleem/, /Sihm/, /Shihm/, /flihm/

2. Increased chanting on B3 exercises to include
   a. Shim +
      1. counting to 12 in groups of 3
      2. using common phrases such as 'what are you doing?', 'what's for dinner?' and 'where are you?'

Update: PP reported that she has been singing in the car along with the radio and is able to sing higher. This transferred into where she felt comfortable doing her exercises. Her single note repeated were on D4 instead of B3. The Woo circle was introduced today. It is a good way to stretch and release the vocal folds without worrying about exact pitches. She was encouraged to draw a circle in the air while using her lips to do the exercise.

Update: Health issues – PP reported that the heel of her right foot is hurting and she believes that she has plantar fasciitis. She will be singing 'Friends' by Michael W. Smith as a duet. We discussed sitting on a stool vs. standing due to her foot. We practiced chanting the text for the song on a comfortable pitch, then sang the harmony part on /floo/, then put text and melody (harmony) together.

Update: PP stated that everything has been fine and that the duet went great and that she was able to stand due to her foot feeling better. We worked on a solo for the women's ministry event. chanting the text on a comfortable pitch, the melody of the verse on /doom/, the melody of the chorus on /shoo/ and then put the two together.

Update: PP stated that she will see an endocrinologist soon in regard to potential thyroid issues.

She stated that she practiced a new duet and that it went well with no fatigue.

Additional exercises

1. more small stepwise patterns joined together
   a. 3-2-1-7-1, 1-2-3-2-1-7-1

2. Worked skipping patterns
   a. 3-1, 1-3-1, 5-3-1, 1-3-5-3-1

3. Worked on the concept of articulation – let the lips and the tongue be in charge of articulation. The jaw gets to relax and flap in the breeze as necessary.

Update: PP reported that she has been diagnosed with hypothyroidism (on the low end of the scale apparently) and that she is waiting for her medications to arrive. She further reported that she has had more stress and noticed breath holding. She started a gluten free diet and her plantar fasciitis has flared up again. We reviewed the concept 'when in doubt blow it out' meaning when she feels stress and notices breath holding to blow air out on /wh/.

Update: PP reported that she will sing another duet soon and also sing with the choir for Christmas Eve. During this session, there was a noticeable improvement in range. She was able to sing from G3 up to B4 for her harmony part in the duet. She reported that her voice has been doing very well. I have encouraged her to practice text three ways: speak (like a monologue), chant, sing.

Case 4: 66-year-old male

LP is a 66-year-old male who has an undergraduate degree in Music Education/Voice and a Masters in Religious Education. LP stated that he enjoys worship leading and getting people involved. He has held positions as church youth music director, Music and young adult ministries and currently is a worship leader and praise band/choir director. The music he directs is a blend of contemporary and traditional worship music. The rehearsals for the band and singers are on Wednesday night from 6-7 pm. The band is comprised of guitar, bass piano, percussion and synthesizer. They have 4 wedge monitors and he uses a wireless microphone at the pedal board with his guitar. After the praise band/singer rehearsal, he rehearses the choir from 7-8pm. On Sunday morning there is a musical run-through starting at 8:30 and the service starts at 9:30 with 20 minutes of music. In addition, he directs a hand bell choir in the Spring and Fall.

LP had his first serious voice problem in 1989 when he was diagnosed with dysphonia caused by a virus. He worked with an Otolaryngologist and Speech and Language Pathologist at the time, to remediate his voice issues.

Surgeries have included: Hernia (1976), tonsillectomy (1977), sinus surgery (2008) and a lumbar L5 and L6 fusion. The first anterior cervical surgery in 2011 was not successful. A year later he had a posterior cervical surgery and it was successful. He noticed a problem with his shoulders post-surgery. He further stated that the voice was fine after the surgery but has noticed issues within the last year. Prior to his surgery in 2012, C4 (middle C) was easy to vocally produce. After the surgery, it was almost not there at all. Along with these surgeries, due to problems with guitar playing he had carpal tunnel surgery in 2013.

When LP started having vocal difficulty, he went to see an otolaryngologist specializing in professional voice care. He was diagnosed with right vocal fold paralysis with incomplete glottic closure creating a gap between his vocal folds during phonation. In 2016, he underwent a surgical procedure called a thyroplasty and a GORE-TEX implant was used for the procedure.

It is important to note that when any surgery is performed that the body, post-surgery, has gone out of homeostasis (where all is balanced) and there is a new normal. What does that mean for LP? That the phonatory system and, in particular, the vocal folds, can look like they are approximating beautifully during the examination procedure of stroboscopy on a single note and can even stretch for range. However, that does not mean that the singer should immediately resume singing, without guidance, what they had been previously singing. Guidance will help the singer to retrain the vocal system's 'new normal' which includes the main body of the vocal folds (thyro-arytenoid muscles), along with a group of the helper muscles (intrinsic laryngeal muscles – cricothyroid, etc.) that must also get comfortable and learn their jobs post-surgery. Singing is an activity that demands fine tuning – correct pitches, agility, range, musicality, not to mention adding text. One must practice text for ease of articulation as well as interpretation of meaning and expression. We discussed the hierarchy of training. There is balance, then consistency, stamina, agility and power.

During his initial singing evaluation LP exhibited shallow abdominal/diaphragmatic breathing, head/neck elevation and protrusion, tongue retraction, an exaggerated vertical movement of his larynx position (pulled up for high pitches and pushed down for low pitches), jaw tension, and neck tension. LP also displayed an extremely tight, compressed base of the neck and high, tight shoulders. He used laryngeal resonance during all phonation while singing.

Exercises recommended

Balance

In order for the vocal folds (VF main body muscle and helper muscles) to learn their new jobs it is beneficial to set up a win-win environment. Although we know that the respiratory system is the power source of the voice, it is necessary to give someone a 'handle to hang onto' at the first session which can be immediately implemented and begin to create balance. The human condition is one of desiring to control. Therefore, if we use an exercise that has safe controllers and takes excessive tension away from the throat then we have a win-win! It is not about making – it is about allowing. The first exercises of benefit to LP include: single note repeated exercises, small patterns and chanting.

1. Single note repeated on pitches D3, Eb3
   a. using /boom-boom-boom-p/

2. Small patterns
   a. 1-7-1, 1-2-1, 3-2-1
   b. using /boom-boom-boom-p/

3. Chanting on a comfortable pitch using Boom +
   a. Song texts

Checklist

- Tongue tip resting behind bottom teeth
- lips – little pucker
- jaw release = duh = let the jaw easily hang
- use little bits of time to practice throughout the day – we do not want to fatigue the new systems balance

Update: LP stated that he is beginning to feel improvement, however it is not consistent.

Additional exercises

Easy onset/off-set using the pairs game

1. Pairs Eb3, D3
   a. /f-v-f/, /s-z-s/, /sh-zh-sh/

2. Longer patterns
   a. 1-7-1-7-1, 1-2-1-2-1, 1-2-3-2-1, 3-2-1-7-1, 1-2-1-7-1, 1-7-1-2-1
   b. Using /boom/, /bloom/, /bleem/, /blihm/

3. Using more variety of consonant/vowel combinations
   a. /flihm-lihm/, /sihm/, /shihm/, /chihm/, /chihm-whim/, /dohm/, /doh/, /flow-low/, /boh/, /low/, /woh/, /wee/, /wih/, /boodley/, /doodley/, /woodley/, /whittley/, /diddley/

4. Pitch Games for freedom of melodic contour
   a. whim

5. Tongue tension release – lizard tongue
   a. with and without sound using bleh

6. Slides using voice/unvoiced pairs
    a. descending, wavy and roller coaster

7. Falsetto slide on /woo/ and /wee/
    1. straight
    2. with one stop and phonate then progress down
    3. with two stop and phonate then progress down

8. 3-2-1
    1. Starting in Falsetto area sliding down
    2. using woo and wee

9. Descendings in pairs with and without nasalant /m/
    /zoo/, /zoom/
    /voo/, /voom/
    /soo/, /soom/
    /choo/, /choom/
    /loo/, /loom/
    /Zih/, /Zihm/
    /Zee/, /Zeem/

Update: LP has felt like he has had a roller-coaster experience of improvement. Some good rehearsal days, some bad. Some good Sunday morning worship leading experiences playing guitar/singing and some not as consistent as he would have liked. Although, from my outside perspective there has been slow, steady improvement. Since LP is in the middle of the inside of the experience, he tends to see only the moment that he is in ... not behind and not where he is headed. Therefore, he has not experienced major improvement until recently. He feels that his resonance and vocal consistency are finally trustworthy. He has been working faithfully on his voice for many months. He started with once a week, moved to every other week, moved to every three weeks and now comes once a month. It was important to remind LP that even though we started 2/2/17 and it is now 12/6/18, he has had a total of 39 session. As a comparison, in college weekly voice lesson land 39 lessons would equal 9.75 months of vocal study. Furthermore, during this time his wife has been very ill, had surgery, was hospitalized and still recuperating. He is happy with his improvement and plans to continue to come to sessions to increase the ease of his upper register.

Case 5: 80-year-old female

JK is an 80-year-old female who is a retired educator and congregational singer. She underwent a partial thyroidectomy and started experiencing breathing problems and hoarseness. She saw an otolaryngologist specializing in voice who diagnosed her with left VF Paralysis post partial thyroidectomy. JK stated that she felt like she is often gasping for breath and has episodes of waking up and not being able to breathe. She was diagnosed with having laryngospasms. She further stated that she is most often very tired. She has also been diagnosed with possible adult onset asthma (reflux?), and severe hearing loss in her left ear. She was referred to the Sound Singing Institute to help with her breathing issues, tension and vocal production.

History at the SSI

JK reported hoarseness post thyroid surgery, shortness of breath, and episodes of gasping for breath. She reported that these episodes would happen 1–2 times in the middle of the night and wake her up. She also stated that she experiences choking on some foods. She stated that the SL-P at the medical office has helped her with swallowing issues and that she has been given medication to calm down her 'episodes.' She reported the following medical conditions: Asthma, allergies, fatigue, thyroid, breathing problems, arthritis, sinusitis. She stated that because of the hoarseness, the otolaryngologist reported that she may need to have a surgical procedure for her voice. The otolaryngologist recommended using a non-permanent procedure first prior to a more permanent procedure such as a Left GORE-TEX® thyroplasty.

It is important to note that at this same time her husband was diagnosed with vascular dementia (she is seeing a counselor), they are looking for retirement places and she was diagnosed with skin cancer on her nose. We discussed the necessity of scheduling ways to relax in her life such as: walks, reading novels, gardening, and getting a massage 1x/mo.

During her initial evaluation JK exhibited extremely shallow clavicular/thoracic breathing, abdominal tension, rib tension, head/neck elevation and protrusion, tongue retraction, jaw tension, and neck tension. It was evident that she often holds her body very still which causes breath holding.

Exercises recommended

1. Airflow – /wh/, /sh/ /s/
   a. sitting
   b. starting bent over and going to straight up sitting slowly
   c. repeat a few times when you think about it, easy/not maximum

2. Discussed doing a 'be good to you' thing daily – reading, gardening etc

3. Schedule: She stated that she needs a daily quiet time in the morning with rest in the afternoon, reading, walking (3/4 mile), patio, flower

4. Discussed the benefit of mental compartmentalizing. The idea is to visualize mailroom mailboxes and to create label for each slot. After working on one of the slots it is necessary to put everything back in that slot prior to thinking about/working on one of the other slots. This technique helps to keep the mind clearer and not so foggy.

Update: When asked, JK reported that she can't breathe through nose because it is sore and stuffy post cancer surgery. She was happy to report that the medication for her 'episodes' is helping tremendously. She only has an episode every now and then.

Additional exercises

1. connected airflow and phonation & Airflow/phonation/resonance
   a. single note repeated on C4

2. using /soo-soo-soop/, /shoo-shoo-shoop/, /soom-soom-soom/, /shoom-shoom-shoom/, /floom-floom-floom/, and /choom-choom-choom/
   b. step-wise small patterns for pitch variation

3. used /choom-choom/ 1-7-1

Update: JK is post GORE-TEX® thyroplasty. She continues to be positive about the benefit of the medication for her episodes. She stated that they are almost totally gone. She did relay that her stress is increasing due to looking at possible retirement housing. JK stated that it needs to be somewhere that has both senior adult apartments and an area where there is assisted living should her husband or she need it at some point. She does not look forward to the notion of packing. We discussed being sure to take time every now and then to blow out on /wh/ to help to reduce her stress level. She reported that she understands the importance of doing this because it helps her to stop holding her stomach and breathe when she is stressed or upset.

Additional exercises

1. Continued with Airflow

2. Single note repeated on A3 and Bb3
    a. using /boom/

3. Chant on A3
    a. /boom/ to /m/ word list – moon, moot, mooch, moose, moat, moan, mean, meander, moment
    b. also use win, wind, window

Update: JK reported that she began to use the reflux medications. We reviewed the importance of when to take them. She also stated that she has come to recognize that it is important for her to have a flexible life plan. JK and her sister have found a retirement place to live which meets all of the required expectations for JK and her husband. Therefore, she is getting ready to pack and move. We discussed the importance of getting help and giving herself permission to take a break when she needs it. We further discussed the concept of using a measured deliberate pace to keep balanced and peaceful. She stated that she would plan to take a moment every hour and check in and relax her stomach.

Additional exercises

1. Continue with previous exercises

2. Remind myself to relax my jaw and throat

3. Sigh on /huh/ 3 x's every now and then

Update: JK reported that she and her husband are in their two-bedroom retirement apartment. They are both very happy, but she has noticed that his dementia is getting worse. She also has to monitor his time on the computer because he is using a credit card and buying many unnecessary things just because he can. She is having to box things up and return them without him knowing to get refunds. Her younger sister has also recently been diagnosed with cancer and will most likely need surgery to remove the tumor. She feels that she has been doing a lot of breath holding due to excessive stress related to her husband and her sister.

Additional exercises

1. Continue with previous exercises
2. Begin pairs exercise Bb3, C4
   a. /f-v-f/, /s-z-s/, /sh-zh-sh/, /th-<u>th</u>-th/

We noticed that she is getting back to a previous pitch area of pre-thyroplasty which is a bit higher. JK stated that there was a potential of taking Tai chi at her retirement center. We reviewed the benefits of body elasticity for her body and breathing. We also reviewed the concept of 'when in doubt blow it out.' We reminded her that when she is tempted to hold back breath, instead keep breathing through whatever you are doing. She tried Yoga but did not like it. She felt that her body/neck and voice too tight after the class. She hopes that the Tai chi will be a good experience.

Update: JK reported that she liked the Tai Chi class however not enough people showed up so they will be going back to offering yoga. We reviewed the important of blowing air out on /wh/. If we start by blowing out, we will get to a place where we need to release and let breath come in. Therefore, we will have a more natural inhalation and will not create stress on the inhale by trying to 'fill-up' with air. The method of 'tanking up' usually results in creating tension on the inhale which is then carried through how breath is used. During exercise, when walking blow out on /wh/ and be sure that your tongue is behind the bottom teeth. Remember that you can also use this when stressed. Just take a moment and blow out on /wh/.

Additional exercises

1. Starting to begin more sustained sounds with single note exercises
   a. /foo----p/
   b. /soo----p/
   c. /shoo----p/

2. Tongue tension
   a. Lizard tongue (tongue in and out) with and without sound – using /bleh/
   b. Tongue side to side

Recently her husband has moved to the care side of the retirement facility. She stated that she is spending time with husband helping the therapists with the arm mobility exercises. She is again noticing breath holding on her part along with jaw tension due to high levels of stress. Her sister also had her surgery to remove her tumor which was successful. Her sister is now undergoing Chemotherapy treatments post surgery. We reviewed the concept of 'when in doubt – blow it out using /wh/. I also recommended that she do gentle body/arm movement while blowing out on /wh/ when she is able. We wrote down reminders of 'let my stomach let go'...

Update: Discussed sitting positions when spending time with her husband. We reviewed how the hips (rock back), lower back relaxes and is not over arched, and the tummy lets go. Further we discussed balanced standing alignment.

Additional Exercises

1. Continue with step-wise patterns
   a. 171,121
   b. increase the length of the patterns using 12171, 17121 321,32171
   c. use /soo/, /foo/, /shoo/

We reviewed voice variables that can cause inefficient voice (what JK refers to as her "croaky" voice)

1. Stress, impacts breath which impacts voice
   a. blow out on /wh/ – nose inhale – warms, purifies and humidifies air

2. The need for humidification
   a. how we can have changes due to environmental external issues, air conditioning, heaters, restaurants, planes

Update: JK continues to work on breathing, her voice and life management. Since we began working together her husband has passed away, she has moved into a one-bedroom apartment unit, and her younger sister has passed away due to the cancer. She is a lovely woman with an indomitable spirit who treasures every day of life. She desires to continue working on her breathing and her voice.

The purpose of this chapter was to share methodology and exercises to help the patient who is experiencing 'new normals'. Hopefully insight has been gained and that those using these exercises will benefit the aging population and all those experiencing 'new normals.'

Recommended exercises page

Preamble

For more information, clarification and figures of the exercises below please see Chapter 2 of the book *The Vocal Instrument* by this author

In regard to the vowels there is a chart for singers trained using the International Phonetic Alphabet (IPA) and a corresponding column in the chart for non-IPA User sounds. Non-IPA is used in this chapter.

IPA vs non-IPA chart examples

IPA	Non-IPA
Fu /u/ (Food)	Foo /oo/ (food)
Fo /o/ (Foam)	Foh /oh/ (foam)
Flo /o/	Flow /oh/
FLIm /I/	Flihm /ih/
Bum /u/	Boom /oo/
BLIm /I/	Blihm /ih/
Bəm /ə/	Buhm /uh/

Relaxation

1. **Duh jaw** – literally let the jaw simply hang like one is thinking/saying /duh/
2. **Lizard tongue** – using /bleh/ with the tongue rapidly moving in and out with or without sound.
3. **Body stretches** – to help create an elastic, responsive system for sound

Sound production systems balance

1. Airflow

a. /huh/ is to be used to relax the breathing system/body – passive exhalation – like an unvoiced sigh, /wh/ is also used to relax the breathing system/body and begin to focus the airflow in an easy manner.

b. /s/, /sh/, /f/ These phonemes are to be used consistently for a comfortable length of time. The objective is consistency of intensity and not for extreme length of time carried out. These sounds belong to a consonant class called 'fricatives' which means a resistance space that airflow travels through. In the case of /s/ and /sh/ it is the tongue position and shape which causes the resistance. In the case of the /f/ it is the teeth on the lip (as well as the lip shape, where the teeth touch on the lip and how much the top teeth touch into the bottom lip). This is used to coordinate the abdominal musculature with steady release of managed airflow using fricative consonants.

s~~~~~~~~~~~~~~ sh~~~~~~~~~~~~~~   f~~~~~~~~~~~~~~

2. Phonation

A. Easy onset/offset

1. Pairs Game: using unvoiced and voiced consonant pairs on a comfortable single pitch
   a. s-z-s (see – zee – see)
   b. sh-zh-sh (shee – zhee – shee)
   c. f-v-f (fee – vee- fee)
   d. th-<u>th</u>-th (think – this – think)

B. Vocal Fold Stretch to release

1. Easy onset/offset slides using unvoiced and voiced consonant pairs
   a. /s-z-s/ (see – zee – see)
   b. /sh-zh-sh/ (shee – zhee – shee)
   c. /f-v-f/ (fee – vee- fee)
   d. /th-<u>th</u>-th/ (think – this – think)

      1. Descending slide

      2. Wavy Slide

      3. Roller Coaster slide

2. Roller Coaster through Falsetto slide
   a. use /woo/ or /wee/

3. Consonant/Vowel combinations – descendings

- This slide is a straight descending slide

- Start with a comfortable pitch and slide down while repeating the consonant/vowel combination of choice *This can also be done starting in Falsetto on /woo/ or /wee/

- Be sure that the tongue tip is behind the front bottom teeth the whole slide (unless you add consonants such as /L/, /ch/, /d/

- Be sure that the center of the tongue does not scoop or press as you go down

- Consonant/Vowel choices
  - Foo, Floo, Floom
  - Foh, Flow, Flowm
  - Flihm
  - Fleem
  - Fweem
  - Choh, Boh, Doh etc.

3. Woo circles

These are used primarily with women's voices to help stretch and release the middle register and to start in the middle register and ascend to upper and back to middle. These are also used as another type of descending exercise of stretch and release. This game helps to increase range and smoothness of shifting registers by keeping the resonance tract in a more or less, consistent shape. Some feel more comfortable going from /woo-woh/ for the upper shift.

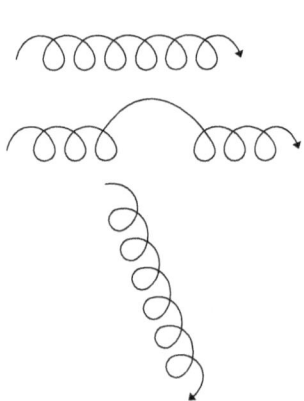

Major scale as a reference

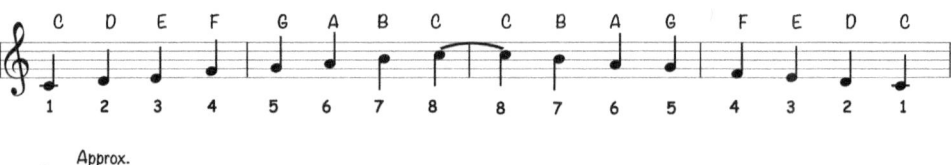

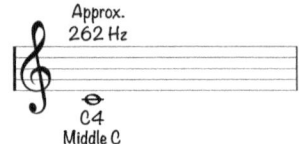

Single Note

Repeated Single note

Stepwise patterns

Stepwise patterns (cont.)

Longer Patterns

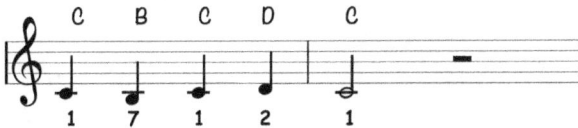

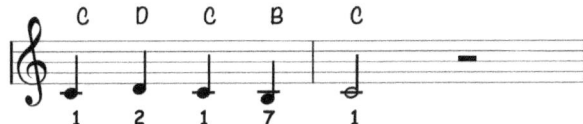

Suggested reading list

Aviv, Jonathan (2014) The Acid Watcher Diet Harmony Books.
Benninger, Michael S., Murry, Johns, Michael M. (2016) The Performer's Voice San Diego, CA: Plural Publishing, 2016.
Bolte Taylor, Jill (2006) My Stroke of Insight New York, NY: Viking Press, Penguin.
Bunch, Meribeth A. (1997) Dynamics of the Singing Voice Vienna: Springer-Verlag.
Christiano, Joseph (1977) Blood types, Body Types and You Lake Mary, FL: Siloam Press.
Doidge, N. (2015) The Brain's Way of Healing New York, NY, Penguin.
Emmons, Shirlee, Alma Thomas (1998) Power Performance for Singers New York, NY: Oxford University Press, 1998.
Gardner, Howard (1983) Frames of Mind New York, NY: Basic Books Inc Basic Books Inc., 1983.
Kaufmann, Jamie, Stern, Jordan, Bauer, Marc (2010) Dropping Acid Sydney: BRIO Press.
Kitt, Eartha with Tonya Bolden (2001) Rejuvinate! (It's Never too Late) New York, NY: Scribner Publishing.
Mitchell, Robert H., Stream, Carol (1993) I Don't Like That Music IL: Hope Publishing Company.
National Association of Teachers of Singing (2013…) So you want to Sing (series) Lanham, MD: Rowman and Littlefield.
Radionoff, Sharon L. (2005) Faith and Voice Portland, OR: Inkwater Press.
Radionoff, Sharon L. (2008) The Vocal Instrument San Diego, CA: Plural Publishing, Inc.
Radionoff, Sharon L. (2011) Where does my Voice Come from? DVD.
Ristad, Eloise (1982) A Soprano on Her Head Boulder, CO: Real People Press.
Sataloff, R.T. (1988) Vocal Health and Pedagogy San Diego, CA: Singular Publishing, Inc.
Sataloff, R.T. (2005) Professional Voice: The Science and Art of Clinical Care 3ed. San Diego: Plural Publishing, Inc.
Sataloff, Robert T., Brandfonbrener, Alice G., Lederman, Richard J. (1998) Performing Arts Medicine San Diego, CA: Singular Publishing, Inc.
Saxon, Keith G., Schneider, Carole M. (1995) Vocal Exercise Physiology San Diego, CA: Singular Publishing, 1995.
Wilson, Frank R. (1987) Tone deaf and all Thumbs New York, NY: Random House.

12

Singing, your brain and memory – Alzheimer's, Parkinson's and Neurogenics

Martha Howe

Neuro-protective benefits

There is a great deal of research ongoing about the effects of music on our brains, our well-being, and on our memory. Making music helps the two sides of our brain communicate with each other, strengthening the bridge between the logical/math/science left side and the creative right side. Because the two sides have to work together, the bridge grows bigger and stronger over time so that musicians' brains have more options for connectivity.

Plus, research shows that singing *or even just thinking about singing*, causes large areas of the brain to light up. To the singer, it feels like a fairly simple thing to do. Something we've done all of our lives. Meanwhile, in our brains, the motor and auditory networks, language, memory, organizational, planning and finally emotional networks all activate. As a final bonus, along with the emotional networks augmenting social bonding and empathy, our reward networks activate sending out dopamine, serotonin, oxytocin, and endocannabinoids. No wonder you feel so much better after singing, and no wonder singing is an integral part of our societal and spiritual rituals.

Singing, playing an instrument, and making music, are all like taking your brain to the gym for a full workout. This continual 'exercising' causes cognitive and structural differences over time. Research shows that when comparing older musicians to the non-musically trained, the musicians have better attention, recall, and reasoning skills.

Add to this, the benefits to the brain of the controlled breathing used in singing. There is a reason that the same kind of breathing is used in meditation, mindfulness, and singing. Focusing your attention on your inhalation and slowing down the exhalation alters the connectivity between parts of your brain and opens up areas of the brain that are normally not accessible. This research is new, so you will be hearing more in the future. Once again, research is catching up to what yogis, meditators, mystics, athletes, and sharp-shooters have been saying for millennia.

We should never underestimate the power of music and song. For example, there are now choirs of homeless people in more and more cities. Singing in these choirs has turned people's lives around, giving them some self-respect and hope, supporting them in their battles with addictions and hopelessness, and giving them purpose, friends, and a support network. They feel seen and valued.

Singing is also proving to be a powerful tool with Parkinson's and Alzheimer's treatments along with other neurogenic disorders caused by stroke and dementia that effect a person's ability to communicate. There is a great deal of research on all these fronts, with new information coming in all the time. One constant has been the positive effects of music and singing.

There are times when a stroke survivor cannot speak, but they can sing. An article by M. Solly in the November 2018 issue of Smithsonian Magazine explores the impressive results of the 'Social Prescribing' projects coming out of England and Canada, where stroke survivors are playing instruments, dance is helping patients with early signs of psychosis, and those with lung conditions are being given singing lessons.

Alzheimer's, music and memory

When a piece of music really hits home, your brain has something called an Autonomous Sensory Meridian Response (ASMR). Because these links to musical memories are relatively undamaged by Alzheimer's, music can sometimes be a pathway through the brain fog. Music certainly can't cure Alzheimer's, but it might make life a bit easier for the patient and for their caregiver. At the time of writing, the Mayo Clinic website includes a list of tips for introducing music and songs to Alzheimer's patients, including singing along with them.

The Alzheimer's Foundation of America has a website dedicated to music therapy and they recommend singing sessions because they activate both sides of the brain. Songs help patients remember every-day activities, and because music is one of the very last things to go, it remains a bridge to the patient and helps manage stress.

Parkinson's treatment and music

Music has become a recognized and valued tool in Parkinson's treatment protocols. The rhythm of a song can aid balance, movement, and stride, while the act of singing helps strengthen the voice, increases volume, and helps with articulation. Since singing and swallowing function share the same muscles, singing helps with swallowing, while humming can help release vocal fold tension.

Group singing helps ameliorate the social isolation, anxiety, and depression common in Parkinson's while improving breathing function, memory and recall. Additionally, singing releases the dopamine and serotonin so beneficial to people with Parkinson's.

Singing, alone or in a group, is one of the greatest gifts you can give to your body. It is not about being perfect, or a wonderful singer, or impressing people with your talent. It is about simply taking air into your lungs, feeling your lungs massage your heart with the inhalation, and letting your heart sing. Your body, your brain, and your heart will thank you for it!

13

What do you do for an encore after the opera is over? Reinventing the female classical voice after menopause

Jennifer Trost

Most classical singers, if they are realistic, anticipate several chapters in a performing career. First there is the education and training phase; secondly, there is the hardest phase, which can take years, of trying to gain experience and make a positive reputation through summer programs and young artist programs; then there is the active performing phase where, if you are lucky, you are either part of a European repertory company or you are able to sustain a constant string of engagements with various American opera companies. Once a performing career begins to wind down, what do you do? Most of us teach, either privately or at a university or conservatory. It's a wonderful privilege to be able to give back to the next, upcoming generation by passing on one's knowledge and experience. However, the question remains, do we continue to sing while teaching full time, or should that end with the active career? If the singing career does continue, how can it be balanced with a teaching career in a productive way?

Transitioning to teaching

After apprenticeships with the Santa Fe Opera and the Los Angeles Music Center Opera (now Los Angeles Opera), I went to Germany and was a soprano soloist for four years with the Wuppertaler Bühnen, in Wuppertal, followed by nine years in the same type of position at the Bavarian State Opera in Munich. Towards the end of my time in Munich, when I was strongly considering moving back home, I decided to teach at the Richard Strauss Conservatory in Munich while still performing at the Bavarian State Opera. Friends back home had told me that, just because I was an opera singer, I shouldn't expect to come back to the United States and be hired on the spot without any prior teaching experience. That's why I decided to lay the groundwork for leaving the performing world and going on into the teaching world by gaining valuable teaching experience at the conservatory.

After three years of teaching at the Richard Strauss Conservatory, I moved back to the United States with a contract to be a visiting professor at the University of California, Santa Barbara, which I did for a year before moving on to The Pennsylvania State University where I have been for the past fourteen years. Penn State is a wonderful place to work because the atmosphere is so harmonious, the colleagues are talented and committed, and the students are a joy to work with. However, one of the things that I had not counted upon was the heavy emphasis on performing as the major part of my research, right up until retirement, which means for me until I am somewhere between 67–70 (much longer than the average performing career for women). That seemed to go against my expectations of what was to happen in the teaching phase of my life and my career. I had thought I would either taper off in my performing or do it at a more reduced level.

Penn State is a major research university and, as such, the faculty is expected to constantly research at a very high level. Since I was hired as a performer, I am expected to sing, and not write articles or books. I have found this difficult, since as I age and begin to experience the effects of menopause, my voice is changing. In addition, because I use my voice all day long in my teaching, I find it hard to practice. I also find it harder to memorize now, compared to when I was younger, and that is a frustration. These are the obstacles I must overcome.

How can I fulfill my obligations and still find fulfillment in my singing? I came to the realization that it was necessary for me to reinvent myself, even considering a *Fach* change by exploring character roles in opera and learning the musical theatre mixed-belt technique to expand my repertoire choices and to promote healthy singing. I was fortunate because I could draw on the expertise of one of my colleagues, Mary Saunders Barton, who is one of the foremost musical theater voice teachers in the country. I turned to her to learn the mixed-belt, which was something quite foreign to me, and to work on improving the transition between my chest voice and head voice. By the way, Mary's position at Penn State centered on teaching and masterclasses for her creative accomplishments, which means that performing was not such an issue for her; it all depends on the expectations contractually agreed upon at the initial hiring.

Challenges

Before I talk about the solutions I have found, let me address the various challenges I, and others in situations similar to my own, must confront. The challenge of having to teach all day and then somehow have enough vocal stamina, physical energy, and mental concentration to perform is quite real. A typical week for me would be teaching either a song literature or opera literature seminar for 1½ hours for two days a week (not to mention preparation time), as well as up to 15 hours of studio teaching, in addition to committee work and administrative duties (I am currently the voice area coordinator). Most of my voice usage is through speaking, since I tend not to model a lot, mainly because my voice is more mature, heavier and more voluminous than those of my students. In adding up the hours of a typical day, I generally start around 9:30 a.m. and finish somewhere between 6:00 – 7:30 p.m. without having had a break (I eat lunch at my computer); I probably work about 4 – 8 hours on school related work on the weekends. With that kind of schedule, there is little time for the practice and memorization required to effectively prepare for a performance.

The other challenge for me, which may be the more important of the two, is the fact that I am over sixty years old and my voice is not what it was twenty years ago, when it was at its peak. Because of physical changes due to menopause, my instrument feels drier now and has shifted downwards in range (although I never was a high soprano). The voice feels heavier and therefore I have lost some agility and the ability to sing coloratura and trills easily. The ability to sing softly is also more of a problem. Some of this is due to the aging process, but some of it is due to the fact that I am singing less regularly. The old adage, 'use it or lose it' is definitely in play here.

Repertoire – then and now

The fact that my voice has a lower range now and less stamina in higher tessituras means that almost all of the repertoire I sang in the past is now unavailable to me. That means that when I do perform, I must learn new material, which in turn takes more time to learn and prepare. I cannot simply fall back on the things I know and freshen them up. It's a much greater time commitment and stress for me wondering if the new repertoire will be all right.

Here's an example of what I mean when I say that the old repertoire is no longer available to me: when I was starting out as a young professional, my go-to aria was Fiordiligi's Come scoglio from Mozart's *Così* fan tutte, K.588. I loved that aria because it gave me a recitative to warm up with and the aria covered a wide range (from A3–C6), while requiring legato, coloratura, and the chance to portray a dramatic situation.

It literally got me my first jobs and opportunities in young artist programs and opera companies:

1. As a resident artist at the Los Angeles Music Center Opera (now Los Angeles Opera)

2. As an apprentice artist with the Santa Fe Opera

3. My first 'fest' position with the Wuppertaler Bühnen in Wuppertal, Germany.

The truth is, I haven't sung this aria in about 25 years. Of course, that is appropriate, since I'm no longer able to, nor do I want to portray a teenaged girl! However, I prepared parts of it to illustrate the changes in my voice as part of my joint presentation with Mary Saunders Barton in 2016 at the National Association of Teachers of Singing (NATS) 54th National Conference in Chicago, Illinois. The challenges that have arisen for me with an aging voice are listed below. I fully expected to demonstrate these shortcomings in the short performance integrated into my presentation at the conference, however, I was surprised when the actual performance went quite well. I think that regular practice and the adrenaline from the moment must have boosted my abilities in that moment!

1. Recitative – the transitions between the head voice and chest voice are more abrupt and harder to negotiate; the sustained B-flat5 at the end is strained and lacks vibrancy.

2. Aria – the wide range from A3-C6 is hard to negotiate; the high C is basically not there anymore.

3. Aria – on the triplet melisma, the voice is not so agile and can only do the figures approximately and at a slower tempo.

4. My former stamina is not there, which makes the end of the aria even harder than it ever was.

Even though I know I will never perform this aria again, part of me wishes that I still could, because I had so much fun singing it in my younger days, and I knew that I could show so much of what my voice was capable of in this one piece. At any rate, this is a good example of not being able to perform the repertoire that I used to sing. I am forced to look for new roles and suitable repertoire; fortunately, this ends up being a good thing, because I want to keep evolving in my profession and in my personal life.

The turbulent 50s

Part of the evolution process means that I have to change my vocal identity, since I am no longer what I once was. That can be very traumatic for a singer, though I have to admit, I was always prepared to accommodate the needs of my voice when the time came. However, it has led me to wonder if I can still call myself a soprano, or if I should change my designation to mezzo-soprano. The problem is that, although the range of the voice has shifted downwards and my chest voice is strong, as it always was, the basic timbre of the instrument is still soprano. What to do?

I guess I never thought I'd really have to deal with the question, because I thought I would just retire from singing and concentrate on teaching. However, being on the faculty of a research university doesn't really allow for that, since it is assumed that one can continue to operate at the same high level as before. I wish that were true, but there are many professions where the body determines the length of the career; think of dance or sports in particular. Any athletic use of the body becomes limited with time and age. Beverly Sills is often used as an example of the fact that female singers in their 50s experience a decline in their abilities. She famously retired at age 50 and then turned her attention to the New York City Opera, serving as their general director (among other endeavors). Women in particular must deal with hormonal changes, often experienced in the decade of the 50's, and these effects on the voice cause us to have to make decisions about how to proceed.

Of course, there are always exceptions to every rule. Some singers are able to preserve their voices and sing to an advanced age. In order to do so, they must choose roles that are suitable for their voices during the various phases of their careers; they need to take care that they do not over-use the voice or come back too soon after illnesses; and they must deal with the hormonal changes, which are different for every individual. These singers often devote themselves and their lives to the craft, no matter the sacrifice. Hopefully their sense of identity is not too closely associated with the success of their careers so that they are able to find happiness in retirement, or in a second career: perhaps teaching voice, being a stage director, or working in arts administration or artist management.

Expectations of a research university

Teaching at a university is my second career, and I have always looked forward to this phase; however, I did not think that the university would have so much difficulty in understanding what I do. The powers that be don't seem to be able to take into account the changes that I am experiencing in my instrument due to aging, nor do they realize what a toll a full teaching load takes on my time, energy, and resources. They also can't imagine how it feels to be an artist, who performed at a high level but is no longer able to do so; the singer's identity is affected at the deepest levels, making it impossible to feel like the same person you once were.

Part of me feels resentful, because I am made to feel like a fish out of water. I often think that a sports analogy would make non-singers understand my situation better. Why didn't Penn State require our iconic football coach, Joe Paterno, to play professional football while he was coaching our team? It seems to me that that would be the equivalent to the expectation made of me or others in my position: if I, as a former opera singer, am required to continue to perform at a high professional level while teaching full time, then a coach and former athlete should have to play at the professional level of his or her sport while coaching. The fact that I must fulfill this expectation, but a coach mustn't, seems to me to be a double standard born of a lack of understanding of the vocal athleticism required to sing opera at an elite level. Additionally, if I were to continue to perform in operas, I'd be gone for four to six weeks at a time and that makes it hard to provide applied students with the necessary mentoring, evaluation and feedback they need on a regular basis.

Jennifer Trost as Elettra in Mozart's *Idomeneo*, K.366 – Wuppertaler Bühnen[1]

So, what should I do – kill myself over it? No, because I have other things to offer at this point in my life: I have a lifetime of experience that informs and deepens what I have to say as an artist. It is still important to stay connected to the spirit of singing.

Speaking voice

Mary and I have had discussions about the importance of developing proper speech habits to assist in sustaining our teaching loads and in assuring good endurance in singing. We've had some wonderful exchanges because Mary, being a musical theatre expert, speaks using thyroarytenoid (chest voice) dominant speech whereas I, the opera singer, use cricothyroid (head voice) dominant speech. To some extent, that means we have chosen to 'live' in different qualities, embracing our chosen professions by how we use our speaking voices. I find that my CT dominated speech helps get me through the day and, in a sense, is modeling for my students, especially those that tend to use vocal fry on a regular basis. We should all be mindful of using an energized and supported voice, no matter the registration.

Hormones

In addition to how one uses the speaking voice, women have to consider whether or not to use hormone replacement therapy (HRT) in the quest to keep the voice in a state closely matching the pre-menopausal voice. Mary and I have made different choices in this area, and each woman must do what works best for her – there is no right or wrong.

She and I both found Barbara Fox DeMaio Caprilli's DMA Dissertation called *The Effect of Menopause on the Elite Singing Voice: Singing through the Storm*[2] to be very insightful in this matter. In it, she elaborates on methods postmenopausal elite singers use to combat declining vocal quality and range. Her study is particularly important because this is a subject that has always been taboo; if a singer admits that she is affected by menopausal changes, it could cause a negative perception of her abilities leading to the loss of marketability and engagements. Caprilli's study seems to indicate that most of the elite singers used HRT or homeopathic equivalents and recommended regular use of the singing voice in a 'use it or lose it' attitude.

Appropriate repertoire

If we are healthy and if we have the desire to continue to sing, then we must find the repertoire that best suits the current version of the instrument. That means that we must seek out age-appropriate opera roles. I find that I love singing Madame de Croissy in Francis Poulenc's *The Dialogues of the Carmelites* or Aunt March in Mark Adamo's *Little Women*. The vocal challenges are minimal, although Aunt March is truly for a contralto, and the acting challenges are fulfilling. In addition, these roles are age appropriate and allow me to interact with younger singers, perhaps even allowing me to serve as a role model for them.

In addition to opera, there is oratorio, although I find that difficult for my voice, since I'm not the high soprano typically favored by these works, and I am not really the contralto they like for contrast with the soprano. That's why I have not chosen to be an oratorio singer, but prefer chamber music, which allows me to be collaborative with my instrumental colleagues. The works are often fairly brief and this allows me to overcome any issues with stamina. The other choice, of course, is to sing recitals. I have to admit, because I have so little time to prepare, I prefer to share a recital with a colleague; a half-recital seems to be the right amount of time to sing and sing well.

Of course, the most interesting choice for repertoire lies in the possibility of commissioning new works, created for your voice and highlighting your positives and hiding your negatives. My current project is a combination of chamber music and opera: Judith Cloud's monodrama – *Beethoven's Slippers* set to a text by Douglas Atwill. It is a work of about 27 minutes and allows me to perform a semi-staged work in either its piano/voice version or in its original piano quartet version. When preparing new works, it is important to choose material that tells your story in the here and now while reflecting your abilities in this phase of your life.

The other possibility, of course, is to look to musical theatre and find appropriate roles in that genre. I have done some work with Mary to try and learn this technique and to help me navigate my chest voice. Some of the roles I thought might be possible for me down the road were Nettie Fowler in Rodger's and Hammerstein's *Carousel* and Ida Straus in Maury Yeston's *Titanic*.

Mixed-belt exercises with Mary Saunders Barton

Some of the most beneficial exercises, from my point of view, that Mary and I worked on to develop and strengthen my voice are listed below (Please see Figures 1–3). She was very patient with me, because I was using my voice in a different way and I could feel the resistance in me when I wanted to take the chest voice higher or use classical vowels instead of those preferred for musical theatre (for instance the /u/ vowel instead of the /ø/ vowel).

Figure 1: Coordinating chest and head dominant resonance

Figure 2: Speak the phrase first, then sing with energy and attitude on the same pitches

Figure 3: Finding a speech-like soprano … think Julie Andrews!

Classical exercises for the chest to head voice transition

In my own teaching, I am currently working with a coloratura soprano, who is over 60 years old and had a nice career, even singing at the Metropolitan Opera. She has many of the issues I have and it's been very interesting to work with her, because as I describe to her the best way to 'freshen up' the voice, I am actually also teaching myself at the same time.

We have used very simple exercises, such as a descending 54321 pattern, first on /i/ and then on /a/ to smooth the transition from head voice to chest voice over the C4 area (Please see Figure 4). We used the /i/ vowel first to keep the forward placement, and then alternated the /i/ and /a/ vowels on every other note to find a universal position for the vowels, and finally put the /a/ vowel in the /i/ placement for greater consistency and to avoid heaviness. This proved to be very effective. (Please see Figure 4).

We also have used exercises with large leaps that go from head voice (much easier than starting with the chest voice) down into the chest voice, and then up again. Usually the problematic vowel was the /a/ vowel, since it wanted to sit too far back and be too heavy. Some examples would be using the 5-1-5 pattern or the 8-1-8 pattern (Please see Figure 5). We would be sure to have the tonic be in the range of C4 to F4, since there was a tendency to take the chest voice up too high. (Please see Figure 5). I rather agree with Nellie Melba in that I prefer not to take the chest voice higher than E-flat4 whenever possible. (For a discussion of the Melba Point, please see Richard Miller's *Training of Soprano Voices*, pages 26, 144, and 145.[3]) Of course, my musical theatre training made me have to confront that point of view, but I think in the opera world, I prefer not to take the chest voice up too high.

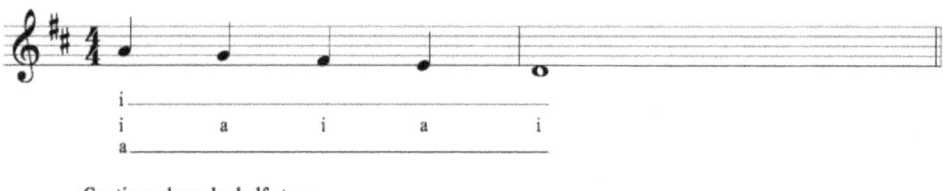

Continue down by half steps.

Figure 4

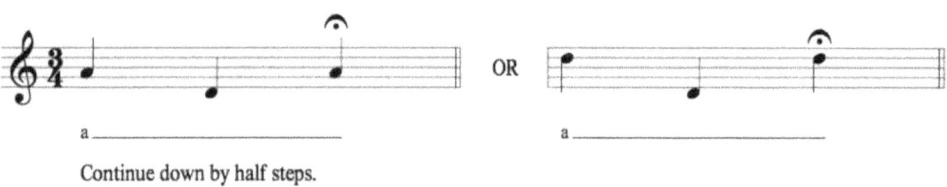

Continue down by half steps.

Figure 5

Exercises for whistle register and highest notes

While working with my over 60-year-old coloratura soprano, we also felt it would be beneficial to examine the high end of the voice and technique. It had been quite a while since she had attempted to access those notes from C6 and above, so we had to approach this range, which had once been the thing that had defined her voice, with patience and gradually restore the expanded range and the confidence she once felt. She often spoke of the feelings she had of being alone in this without anyone to turn to. Once she started taking voice lessons, she felt that she had an advocate and this gave her a very positive psychological boost; having a teacher at this phase of her singing life was important, not only to rework her technique, but to relearn to sing with confidence and to find the joy in singing again.

What was perhaps the hardest step was making her realize that she had to sing with the present instrument and not to mourn the younger version of this same voice. We had to find a neutral state, free of judgement, so that we could move forward. Of course, what we discovered in building a more reliable instrument for her was the fact that 'use it or lose it' was very much in effect here. In addition, becoming reacquainted with her voice and developing her awareness of the muscular coping mechanisms she had developed over time was key. She had started to retract her tongue, perhaps in order to try to lower the larynx, and she did a lot of pulling down of the lips and mouth, again to try to relax tensions that had crept in. We found that releasing the tongue and adding lift to the palate really helped her find the balance she had been missing. She found a great deal of freedom and release, which allowed her to sing healthily and consistently in what I would call a more technically correct manner.

This progress allowed us to examine the flageolet register, which had been hampered by an overly muscular use of the tongue. She told me that it was helpful for her to do exercises on the 'u' vowel and that bringing the whistle register lower than she normally would into the G5-C6 range really helped her to recalibrate the upper extremes and allowed her to disengage her tongue. Some of the exercises we did are shown in Figures 6, 7 and 8, listed below.

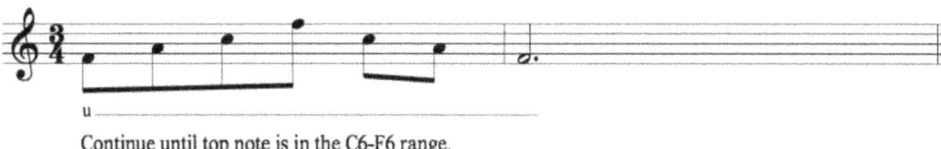

Continue until top note is in the C6-F6 range.

Figure 6

Continue until top note is in the C6-F6 range.

Figure 7

Continue until top note is in the C6-F6 range.

Figure 8

Breath and vibrato

The other aspect of technique that we had to examine together was the interrelated nature of breath and vibrato. Her vibrato had become quite slow and wide. Our work focused on preventing her from holding and encouraged her to let go and allow the air to flow and spin, while learning to trust this approach. She had somehow acquired an aggressive approach, which made her hold, rather than release the air, thus causing secondary tension in the throat. We had to reestablish stability, balance, and release. We found that continuous energy and 'spinning' support helped her to develop a flexible firmness and avoid the feeling of being locked up. When I asked what seemed to help most, she said, "Air, air, and more air". In other words, she was not trying to over-produce, but rather was able to allow the continuity and flow to carry her through without adding anything extraneous to the process. This work also helped her to create a true legato.

The exercises we did to address the breath and vibrato issues were often vocalizes created from excerpts from the repertoire she was performing in the studio. In addition, we did some messa di voce exercises and moving exercises encouraging flow and agility. (Please see Figures 9–10).

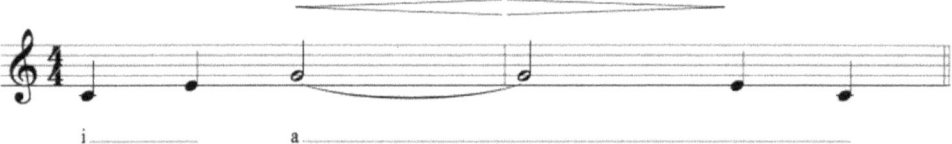

Figure 9

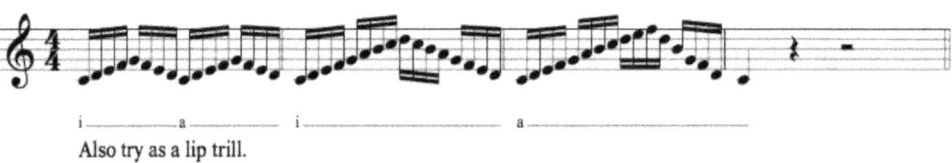

Also try as a lip trill.

Figure 10

It has been a very satisfying and vicarious experience to help restore this voice and to observe the joy that this singer has found once again in her voice and her singing. In many ways, the most important aspect of our work together was to create a safe, non-judgmental place where she could learn to embrace the current version of her voice; once that was accomplished, she was able to move on and make quick technical progress while experiencing an accompanying sense of well-being. This break-through has allowed her to work again at a very high level and I'm personally glad that we have not lost this valuable musician, who has so much more to say.

Conclusion

For me, I had to make some honest assessments of myself in order to combat the aging process, embrace it, and work with it. Once I determined that I needed to practice and sing regularly, or in other words incorporate the 'use it or lose it' philosophy, I needed to make sure that other areas in my life were in balance. I've always been good at hydrating, so that is no problem. I think that my technique is basically healthy, although I notice my tongue wanting to retract more than it ever did – it's probably trying to help me support in some way, so I need to make sure that the work isn't going to the wrong place and just be mindful of it. I think paying attention to diet and physical exercise is also important. If you are healthy physically in other areas, the voice will often follow.

The non-physical areas are just as important. Finding projects that are of interest to you and which offer enjoyment for you is the biggest priority. Being open to alternative types of repertoire (like musical theatre for me) can present new outlets for expression. It's also important not to be afraid to find a new identity for yourself as a singer and thereby reinvent yourself. The harder part might be the temptation to mourn the loss of your previous self as a singer. It's important to acknowledge change and to embrace this phase in your life and career as an opportunity to evolve – staying open to all possibilities and trying things out to see what works for you. Keep a sense of purpose in your life and continue your life-long joy of singing. It can enable you to continue to sing, particularly if you're willing to care for your voice and to allow your identity as a singer to evolve.

Acknowledgements and references

Jennifer Trost as Elettra in Wolfgang Amadeus Mozart's *Idomeneo*, K.366 – Wuppertaler Bühnen (1991). Photo by Uwe Stratmann Fotografie, Völklingerstrasse 6a, D-42285 Wuppertal, Germany.
Fox DeMaio Caprilli, Barbara. *The Effect of Menopause on the Elite Singing Voice: Singing Through the Storm*. DMA Dissertation, Shenandoah Conservatory, Winchester, VA, 2013.
Miller, Richard (2000) *Training Soprano Voices*. New York, NY: Oxford University Press.
Edward Barton for his transcriptions of vocal exercises #1-3 using the Finale Music Notation Software.

Matthew Anthony Tiramani, Graduate Assistant in Music Technology and Music Composition, The Pennsylvania State University, for his transcriptions of vocal exercises #4-8 using the Finale Music Notation Software.

A helpful resource for me was Mary Saunders Barton's 2007 DVD, *Bel Canto Can Belto: Teaching Women to Sing Musical Theatre* produced by Penn State Public Broadcasting.

This chapter is based on a joint presentation with Mary Saunders Barton at the National Association of Teachers of Singing (NATS) 54th National Conference on July 10, 2016 in Chicago, IL

14

Keep singing and pay attention to your speaking

Martha Howe

Aging is not a disease. We start the journey of aging from the moment we are born, then our overall health and genetics are major players in how that journey will affect the voice. The inevitable changes along the way can become lessons in forced adaptation from our bodies, or bothersome obstacles to overcome, or roadblocks that stop us in our tracks. Perhaps they will be all three. However severe or merely bothersome these changes are, this process is facilitated by viewing it as dancing lessons from our aging body and focusing on adapting to what's happening in the present rather than resisting the changes and living in the past.

We tend to do what we are good at, and avoid what is new, different, or challenging. Often, as things get difficult, we simply stop doing them. Sometimes this is conscious, sometimes unconscious. It can be very challenging later in life to reopen doors we have closed, to start a new venture, and to go back to being a beginner. It is also extremely rewarding and recommended as exercise for our brains.

If you want to avoid the weaker, scratchier, 'old-person' speaking voice, sing regularly. Singing is like exercise for your speaking voice and, just like all exercise, becomes much more important as the decades roll on. It will help maintain and build stronger breath and more warmth and energy in your speaking voice. There are wonderful semi-occluded vocal exercises all through the chapters in this book, because they work. Try them!

Whether or not you are taking voice lessons, whether your focus is on singing or speaking, it is recommended to exercise the full range of the voice. There is no one magic-bullet exercise, as everyone is different with individual needs and expectations.

However, 'sirening' without tension and with sufficient moving air, is a proven favorite. To ameliorate the results of the aging process, we need to preserve our neural-muscular activity and agility. Regular, healthy, easy singing with a focus on what your breath is up to, will help you with strategies for maneuvering through the vocally rough or gravelly patches that often develop in older voices.

Keep in mind that you speak much more than you sing, so it is wise to pay attention to how you are speaking. Is your voice getting softer all the time? Is your breathing getting more shallow? Are you speaking less? Or have some of the people around you become hard of hearing, and you find you need to speak louder and louder? This can be very tiring, can sound angry, and still may not be getting across to the hard of hearing. All of these variations will affect your voice.

If your voice is rough or you are having trouble being heard, it is well worth your time to go to a Speech Language Pathologist (SLP), especially one familiar with the Stemple Voice Function Exercises. Even five or six sessions with them will be helpful and effective. They are a great resource for dealing with the changes aging brings to the voice.

Remember the difference between 'shout' and 'call'. If someone is doing something you think is dangerous, how do you tell them to stop? (Most often a 'barking', commanding, shout.) If you have a favorite pet, how do you call their name? (Most often a lilting, head voice, call.) There are exercises to help strengthen 'call' in the chapter "Hearing, Sliding Pitch, Wobble, and Hitting the Gravel". 'Call' lets the voice rise naturally into a slightly higher, clearer, placement and is easier both to produce and to listen to. It can be a mistake to try and just raise the pitch of your voice, as that can easily become strident and not very comfortable. The landmarks of 'call' are that it is comfortable with little or no tension, doesn't tire the voice, is clear, and easy to listen to.

Although it feels like you are losing pulmonary function (the ability to get a good breath and sing a long phrase), much of that is coordination and confidence. Get walking, gently swing your arms and move your torso, or dance around your living room, anything that will increase your cardio exercise and get you breathing, will have a positive effect, and you feel the improvement. The SOVT exercises are great for strengthening and balancing your exhalation. Working with yoga or Pilates instructors who understand breath and incorporate breathing into the movements will also help. You still have the same pulmonary capacity (unless you've been smoking or fallen prey to a lung disease), but as we slow down and our overall energy level lowers, we breathe more conservatively. Our voices depend on the air flow over the vocal folds for sound, and when that weakens so does the voice.

There are many ways to have fun beyond singing along with the radio or iTunes, in the shower, the car, and while cooking:

Join a choir: Choirs are full of interesting people, and a great reason to get out of the house, be challenged, and socialize. There are many types of church or synagogue choirs and various types and levels of community choirs. Some of these choirs require auditions but many do not. Look around and find a group where you feel comfortable with the people, the conductor, the pace of the rehearsals, and the style of music. Then settle in and enjoy the music, the unity, and the fun!

Sing-along evenings: Gather a group of friends together once a week, or every other week, to sing together for fun. If you have a pianist, gather around their piano. If you have a guitarist, you can meet in different members' homes.

- Pick someone to be responsible for providing sheet music for the pianists or lead sheets for guitarists and providing sheet music or lyric sheets for the singers.

- One person can be responsible for choosing and providing all the music and/or lyric sheets.

- Or you can have one person host and another person choose the music, rotating these responsibilities around the group.

- "Stone soup" evenings are fun when everyone brings something to share and the beverage of their choice.

- Explore what works in your group.

Group and solo karaoke: There is an ocean of karaoke songs. Old ones, new ones, camp songs, great American songbook, musicals, opera, old sentimental favorites, country, you name it, it's probably there somewhere. There are karaoke nights at restaurants, bars, etc., that range from serious karaoke singers to embarrassed beginners. The books of songs tend to be listed by song title or by artist and are fun to leaf through for inspiration. Many karaoke tunes are available online and on YouTube so you can see what you are getting into and try different versions out in the privacy of your living room before venturing out. Try singing along with it to get used to the speed, the key, and holding the melody by yourself. This alone is wonderful vocal exercise and a lot of fun.

The people who sing karaoke on a regular basis buy their own karaoke players and karaoke CDs or downloads, which have the graphics of the words. Karaoke at-home machines range from kids' toys to the more sophisticated players that will let you adjust the tempo and transpose up and down to find a more comfortable key. These will also connect to your television screen for easy reading of the lyrics. You will feel much more confident if you sing to versions that you know and have practiced.

Karaoke is grand fun as part of an evening out, at home alone with your computer, or together in a group with friends or family. There are so many wonderful, favorite songs out there waiting to be sung!

You can do it!

It is said that the voice is a reflection of what is going on in your emotions and your health. There is new research on using voice prints to diagnose changes in health, and the ancient art of healing with sound is returning. The people who manage elite vocalists have a saying that "Unhappy birds do not sing." With all of the research on how singing releases serotonin, dopamine, oxytocin, and the endocannabinoids, it would seem that if that bird wishes to cheer up, it should start singing. There comes a time when it is no longer wise to focus on and keep trying to do what you **can't** do any longer, and better to turn your attention to enjoying what you **can** do.

So, make the time to sing. In the car, in the shower, to the radio, with your playlists, while you walk, to your pets, when you cook, while you play with your grandkids, to your beloved, or whenever the mood strikes. It doesn't need to be perfect, perfection can be boring. You are much more aware of your flaws and foibles than anyone else is, they are generally busy fussing over their own flaws and foibles. Loosen up your shoulders and neck, relax your jaw and tongue, take a sweet, life-affirming breath, and let your voice flow. Your body will thank you!

www.ingramcontent.com/pod-product-compliance
Lightning Source LLC
Chambersburg PA
CBHW082149300426
44117CB00016B/2670